Corporate Social Responsibility

PARTNERS FOR PROGRESS

OECD

ORGANISATION FOR ECONOMIC CO-OPERATION AND DEVELOPMENT

ORGANISATION FOR ECONOMIC CO-OPERATION AND DEVELOPMENT

Pursuant to Article 1 of the Convention signed in Paris on 14th December 1960, and which came into force on 30th September 1961, the Organisation for Economic Co-operation and Development (OECD) shall promote policies designed:

- to achieve the highest sustainable economic growth and employment and a rising standard of living in Member countries, while maintaining financial stability, and thus to contribute to the development of the world economy;
- to contribute to sound economic expansion in Member as well as non-member countries in the process of economic development; and
- to contribute to the expansion of world trade on a multilateral, non-discriminatory basis in accordance with international obligations.

The original Member countries of the OECD are Austria, Belgium, Canada, Denmark, France, Germany, Greece, Iceland, Ireland, Italy, Luxembourg, the Netherlands, Norway, Portugal, Spain, Sweden, Switzerland, Turkey, the United Kingdom and the United States. The following countries became Members subsequently through accession at the dates indicated hereafter: Japan (28th April 1964), Finland (28th January 1969), Australia (7th June 1971), New Zealand (29th May 1973), Mexico (18th May 1994), the Czech Republic (21st December 1995), Hungary (7th May 1996), Poland (22nd November 1996), Korea (12th December 1996) and the Slovak Republic (14th December 2000). The Commission of the European Communities takes part in the work of the OECD (Article 13 of the OECD Convention).

FOREWORD

The role of business is rapidly changing. In today's emerging global society, businesses have embraced corporate social responsibility (CSR) as a value reflective of their new role in contributing to societal goals, but also as a strategy for improving the bottom line. Increasingly, business seeks to maintain corporate identity while at the same time upholding social and environmental standards and confronting the concerns of social exclusion and community development. Recent events such as the Lisbon Summit of the European Union in March of 2000, the United Nations Global Compact, and the OECD Guidelines for Multinational Enterprises highlight the importance of the role and limitations of corporations in policy making.

On 15 November 2000, the OECD LEED Programme (Local Economic and Employment Development) and the Philip Morris Institute, jointly organised a Roundtable Conference '*Partners for Progress - Towards a New Approach to Corporate Social Responsibility*'. Approximately 130 representatives from the private sector, non-governmental organisations, and local and central government came together to better define corporate social responsibility, to discuss how companies, including SMEs, can partner together and with governments and civil society actors to tackle unemployment, social exclusion, barriers to entrepreneurship and to share experience in financing such public/private partnerships.

Special thanks to Giles Merritt and his team of the Philip Morris Institute and Forum Europe for their co-operation in this project.

This publication was drafted by Shari Nourick, consultant to the OECD LEED Programme, under the management of Sergio Arzeni.

This book is published on the responsibility of the Secretary-General of the OECD.

TABLE OF CONTENTS

Boxes

INTRODUCTION

Keynote Address

Donald J. Johnston, Secretary-General of the OECD

I would like to give a warm welcome and say it is a privilege to have you here at the OECD and to thank the Philip Morris Institute for helping sponsor the event and Mr. Merritt for his participation. I think that this is going to be a very interesting day because you are focusing on issues that are extremely important, including for the work of the OECD. Social progress and sustainable development depend very much on balancing achievements with respect to growth, social cohesion and good governance.

'Globalisation' is the integration of our national economies largely through trade and investment, but also through the flow of ideas, people, capital, and technology. This has tremendous potential to develop new growth and jobs. The analysis done in the OECD demonstrates that measurable wealth has been created through increased trade and investment. However, I do not see globalisation as a policy. No one has said, 'we want to globalise'. Rather it is an irreversible process, and at the heart of that process of course is business. The expansion of international business, supported by information communication, technology, transportation and so on, is driving economic integration. It is a process, and our task is to manage that process and to help shape globalisation for the benefit of all. This is an underlying rationale for most of the activities of the OECD.

If globalisation brings such benefits, why are we seeing at the same time so much resistance to it? Why do we see demonstrations, such as at Seattle, Washington, Prague? I had the privilege of being at each of these events and talking to some of the demonstrators. I do not think that their issues are at the heart of concerns about globalisation. Of course they capture a lot of media attention and contribute to the impression of resistance. But the real concern is about people who are perhaps being left behind. Although there is no doubt that globalisation is creating wealth, many may feel that it hasn't brought wealth to them, or to their friends and family. 'Globalisation may all right for Wall Street, but it is not doing a great deal for Main Street'.

One of the great challenges for us here at the OECD is to ensure that policies help guarantee that wealth will be shared. This happens in many, many ways. It happens through economic development that creates good, well paying jobs, and it happens through the fiscal system. Jobs are the best way of sharing this wealth. Benefits to consumers are another. Consumers today enjoy lower prices and more choice thanks to globalisation. I argue that economic policies must have a social objective and when I came to the OECD, I introduced what I call the triangular paradigm: anchored in one corner by economic growth, in the other by social cohesion and social stability, and the linchpin of course is good governance. In the absence of any one of these, the full benefits of globalisation will not be realised and shared, and in fact it will come to a stop.

The OECD Member governments all have been working diligently in OECD to support globalisation in a number of ways. Let me just touch upon a few of them:

- The Trade Committee of the OECD is extremely active and the work we do in this Committee supports the work of the World Trade Organisation (WTO). The Trade Committee is addressing new issues that become increasingly important: trade and environment, trade and labour standards or trade and competition policy. It has had great successes in the past and I can refer to the issue of agriculture in the Uruguay Round. Agriculture was and remains a difficult subject, with each country having different mechanisms of income support, price support, etc. The OECD created what are called the producer subsidy equivalents and consumer subsidy equivalents that allowed all the various forms of subsidisation to be quantified in a comparable manner. It was quite a remarkable achievement that was accepted within the OECD and the WTO and it is now the benchmark that is used to measure progress in reducing trade protection in agriculture.

- The OECD is also extremely active in international investment. You probably all know about the MAI (the Multilateral Agreement on Investment) and the failure of that negotiation. That however, did not stop foreign investment by companies from OECD countries, because investment is an absolutely critical part of globalisation.

- The OECD is central to international competition policy and has played an important catalysing role in promoting co-operation among national competition agencies. Formally, its efforts have borne fruit in the form of two OECD Council Recommendations in 1995 and 1998. The OECD has also been engaged in constructing building blocks for closer co-operation between the trade and competition policy communities. These building blocks are useful in stimulating the development of the common approaches to be incorporated into multilateral competition agreements.

- Taxation is another area that is absolutely fundamental to globalisation. With multinational enterprises controlling so much of the trade, inter-corporate trade becomes critical. When a component is manufactured in one tax jurisdiction, incorporated in an intermediate product in a second and shipped for final assembly to a third jurisdiction, how does one ensure that each one of the countries receives its fair share of the tax? The OECD Transfer-Pricing Guidelines serve as a model that is applied internationally, and they have been updated within the last four years.

- The OECD is at the centre of the work being done on electronic commerce. Government representatives come here to work together on issues like consumer protection guidelines, cryptology, and questions concerning science and technology that bear upon e-commerce. The OECD also facilitates work with other participants such as the World's Custom Union, United Nation agencies, business associations, international consumer associations, or other non-governmental organisations. They are interested in encouraging the use of e-commerce.

I do not want to give you a *résumé* of all the work we are doing at the OECD, because so much of our work is related to globalisation.

I should emphasise that these questions can not be restricted to consideration by just OECD Member countries. Each one I have mentioned is a global issue and OECD is bringing non-member countries into all these activities.

It is important that the benefits of globalisation be widely shared. Corporations and their social responsibility, which you are going to discuss today, is considered a global issue, but has local applications everywhere -- you can think globally, but you have to act locally, certainly in this area. It is fundamental and this is why we do so much work with the business community, ranging from SMEs to large multinational enterprises. Each has to assume new and perhaps different responsibilities in the world today. We talk about corporations as if they are people, but they are not. The corporations are operated by their management and shareholders and reflect the ideals that these people have. Thus when I talk about corporate social responsibility, I am looking through that corporate veil to the men and women who direct those corporations and who must embody responsibility. That is why the leadership and the ethics of these corporations are so critical. I think that this goes from the smallest corporation to the largest corporation and this has become a subject of much discussion in the last few years.

There are differences with respect to corporate governance within the OECD but we have developed the OECD Principles of Corporate Governance as a base or reference point that reaches right across the OECD. This was a major achievement, because you may think that the OECD is a group of like-minded countries and like-minded societies, and to a large degree that is true in terms of values, but in terms of culture and tradition, there are tremendous differences within the OECD. There are Anglo-Saxon models, European models and so on, and we were able to succeed in developing a set of core principles. This was made possible due to the men and women from all walks of life, from various responsibilities, corporations, stock exchanges, throughout OECD Membership, and NGOs who participated actively to see if these core principles could be developed. They cover a full set of relationships between a company's management, its boards, its shareholders, and its other stakeholders, such as the communities in which corporations are located or in which they do business. Issues such as disclosure, and transparency, as well as others are covered in the guidelines. Indeed, the World Bank saw these as being significant globally, and while the guidelines were developed largely in the OECD Membership, it was obvious that these same core principles should apply to governance throughout the world. In particular, good corporate governance attracts foreign direct investment, and thus these guidelines are seen as pivotal to the developing world and to the emerging market economies who, if they adopt these principles, will be much more likely to receive strong influx of investment.

The OECD organises international roundtables that bring together government officials and members of the business community to examine these principles. These are not just 'one off events', but an ongoing activity. The importance of these roundtables was brought home to me when I was in China last year. The Chinese had taken these principles of the OECD and translated them into Chinese and told the business community that these were the world standard and that they would need to adhere to them in order to continue to attract the kind of foreign direct investment that they needed. This is one contribution to the issue on corporations and social responsibility.

Another more recent example was an updating of the codes of conduct governing multinational enterprises that were adopted with some difficulty at the OECD Ministerial last June. When I say with some difficulty I mean that in a positive way, because there was thoughtful debate and discussions taking place. The international business community and various countries involved took these very seriously because we were strengthening not only the guidelines, but also the procedures for implementation. They represent codes of conduct to which corporations should adhere and to which they should be held accountable.

We have been very fortunate, since from the outset the OECD has had the benefit of input from the OECD Business Industry Advisory Council (BIAC) and also the Trade Union Advisory Board (TUAC), led today by John Sweeney of the AFL-CIO. Thus, we have the capacity to bring all of the major stakeholders together and discuss candidly the importance of issues like corporate social responsibility and the application of these guidelines. It is one thing to develop guidelines, and it is another thing to apply them. This is the kind of challenge we have in countries like Russia, where issues on governance can be put into laws through legislature, but unless guidelines get translated into action and applied, they are meaningless. It takes systems and people to accomplish good governance and the same thing is true with corporate social responsibility. We can have lofty ideas, but these need to be distilled at one point into concrete action and concrete examples in the various communities in which these corporations operate.

So, Mr. Chairman, I wish you a very fruitful day and I am very pleased that you are here. I am leaving you with experts from the OECD who are more familiar with this area, certainly at the LEED Programme, than I myself am. I thank you very much and I wish you great success and I am looking forward to hearing the results of these deliberations.

PART 1

CORPORATE SOCIAL RESPONSIBILITY IN A GLOBAL ECONOMY

Overview of discussions

Corporate Social Responsibility (CSR) is high on the policy agenda of OECD governments. CSR can mean different things to different groups, sectors, and stakeholders. But there is general agreement that in a global economy, businesses are often playing a greater role beyond job and wealth creation and CSR is business's contribution to sustainable development. Consequently, corporate behaviour must not only ensure returns to shareholders, wages to employees, and products and services to consumers, but they must respond to societal and environmental concerns and values. The notion of CSR is a holistic concept and it is an evolutionary process emerging in many different directions. This holistic approach must provide mutual benefits to society as a whole as well as business, and corporations need to manage CSR as any other part of their business strategy. Corporations are faced with a triple bottom line, to advance economically, as well as being environmentally and socially responsible. The growing role of business in social and economic development is expected to continue. CSR has now become a major component of university business courses in both the United States and Europe and most OECD-based multinational enterprises have participated in the area of corporate responsibility in one way or another.

> '*Business decisions can profoundly affect the dignity and rights of individuals and communities...It is not a question of asking business to fulfil the role of government, but of asking business to promote human rights in its own competence.*'

Mary Robinson, 1998,
UN High Commissioner for Human Rights.

Why should companies be socially responsible?

The first part of the Roundtable focused on the question of how to define what a socially responsible company is and what a company does to be considered socially responsible. Even before answering that question, some might ask why a company should be considering this issue. The answer is tied to globalisation. Globalisation is not just about closer ties between nations, but concerns processes, and the result is the emergence of a global civil society. The world has changed due to globalisation and with this the business climate and attitudes have changed as well. With globalisation and the fall of the communist system in the 1980s, business worldwide began to respond to new challenges. Solutions to social problems were to be found within the free market system and business. The old ideas of maximising profits and concentrating all concerns on shareholder interests are evolving and the interests of all stakeholders need to be considered in today's global economy. Globalisation has altered the internal and external power relations between and within companies, and in the community as a whole, and society has turned to business to engage in finding solutions to this complex phenomenon.

At the same time, in the late 1980s, the debate on corporate governance gathered momentum in the United States and in the United Kingdom, mostly in response to corporate collapses, corporate raiders and destabilising mergers and acquisitions, as well as business fraud and corruption. Globalisation and the market were placing power in the hands of the private sector, but public distrust in the reliability and honesty of corporations was high and widespread. Issues of accountability, monitoring and disclosure, standard setting and globality were key to the debate. It became clear that companies could no longer manage the effects of their business practices simply by paying taxes and complying with national regulations. They are expected to take on greater responsibilities for managing their impact on society.

Rules for corporate social responsibility: some examples

Implementing social responsibility is facilitated through standards and common codes of conduct. While firms themselves have set the standards, governments have played a role in defining common rules. Codes of conduct were created and emerged internationally, providing principles for business that promote benchmarking issues for human rights, workplace safety, transparency, environmental management, consumer protection and fighting corruption. Initiatives like the Caux Round Table and the UN's Global Sullivan Principles were conceived with the goal of building a platform for international solidarity for corporate responsibility on the global level. The Global Reporting Initiative (GRI) established *Sustainability Reporting Guidelines* in June 2000, representing a major step toward a generally accepted global framework for sustainability reporting. The GRI aims to provide a management tool to help the reporting organisation evaluate and continuously improve its performance and progress. Even more recently, in November 2000, the Voluntary Guidelines on CSR Communicating were adopted in Brussels and supported by the European Union, encouraging companies to undertake voluntary reporting across company operations.

Box 1. The Caux Round Table and the Global Reporting Initiative

The Caux Round Table (CRT) is a network of senior business leaders from both industrialised and developing nations. The CRT was initiated in 1986 in Caux, Switzerland by current and past CEOs and senior executives that seek to make a practical impact, assuring that developing nations share in the benefits of economic globalisation. The CRT is not a single-issue organisation, but pursues a broad visionary and catalytic role in its relationship to global issues. The CRT offers business leaders a forum for dialogue, a way to co-operate in order to make a positive difference, and allows for reviewing and monitoring outcomes.

A different approach is taken by the Global Reporting Initiative GRI). Convened in 1997, GRI is an international multi-stakeholder effort that creates a common framework for voluntary reporting of the economic, environmental, and social impact of organisation level-activity. The GRI incorporates the active participation of businesses, accountancy, human rights, environmental, labour, and governmental organisations. GRI is a disclosure framework based on reporting principles, characteristics and indicators. GRI promotes international harmonisation in the reporting of relevant and credible corporate performance information to enhance responsible decision-making.

The OECD Guidelines for Multinational Enterprises, revised in 2000, comprise recommendations from 33 governments to multinational corporations covering issues such as humans' rights and environmental protection. They are the only multilaterally endorsed comprehensive code of conduct that governments are committed to promoting and the business community was also an active participant in updating the Guidelines for today's global world. Most codes of conduct are aimed at suppliers and not necessarily workers and stakeholders, but these new Guidelines give greater attention to consumers' rights and calls on companies to provide accurate and clear information on products and to effectively address consumer complaints. While it is essentially up to participating governments to reform systems and promote and monitor the implementations of the Guidelines, the continued co-operation from business will be extremely important in achieving the Guideline's objectives. It is clear that if wholly implemented, the Guidelines would help ensure that multinational enterprises contribute considerable benefits to the localities in which they operate for sustainable economic and social development. These guidelines, as well as the others, have an important role to play in the ongoing process of corporate social responsibility, strengthening worldwide commitment and encouraging consensus building and the dissemination of knowledge.

Box 2. The OECD Guidelines for Multinational Enterprise

The OECD Guidelines for Multinational Enterprises (MNEs) were first issued in 1976 and were revised in 2000 to bring them up to date in the rapidly changing global economy. The OECD Guidelines for MNEs establish voluntary policies that promote corporate transparency and accountability, specifically addressing disclosure of material information, employment relations, environmental management, bribery, competition, consumer interests, and science and technology diffusion.

Implementation of the Guidelines is facilitated by the key government institution responsible, the National Contact Points (NCPs). NCPs undertake promotional activities, gather information and assist in problem solving. Each NCP will submit an annual report of its activities to the OECD's Committee on International Investment and Multinational Enterprises (CIME).

The revised Guidelines emphasise that the recommendations represent good practice wherever enterprises operate, and not just within the OECD area. Although the Guidelines are not legally binding, the latest version strengthens signatory governments' responsibility for promoting and implementing them, and these Guidelines are the only comprehensive code of corporate conduct agreed to by multiple nations.

In 1999, at the Davos World Economic Forum in Switzerland, The U.N Secretary-General, Kofi Annan challenged business leaders to join a 'global compact' of shared values and principles and give globalisation a human face. He argued that unless the global market was held together by shared values, it would be exposed to backlashes from protectionism, populism, nationalism and even terrorism. The UN Global Compact is based on 9 principles covering topics in human rights, labour and environment. World business was asked to:

- **Principle 1**: support and respect the protection of international human rights within their sphere of influence;
- **Principle 2**: make sure their own corporations are not complicit in human rights abuses;
- **Principle 3**: uphold freedom of association and the effective recognition of the right to collective bargaining;
- **Principle 4**: uphold the elimination of all forms of forced and compulsory labour;
- **Principle 5**: uphold the effective abolition of child labour;
- **Principle 6**: uphold the elimination of discrimination in respect of employment and occupation;
- **Principle 7**: support a precautionary approach to environmental challenges;
- **Principle 8**: undertake initiatives to promote greater environmental responsibility;
- **Principle 9**: encourage the development and diffusion of environmentally friendly technologies.

The Secretary-General asked corporations to uphold and enact these principles in their individual corporate practices and by supporting appropriate public policies. The initiative was instantly criticised as inadequate, because there is no monitoring device, however businesses from every continent, ranging from the world's largest banks to small train companies in India, have pledged to support and implement the principles. The Global Compact Principles are helping to develop a dialogue between global trade union organisations and corporations worldwide. In January of 2001, two years after the original Global Compact speech in Davos, Kofi Annan named Mr. Göran Lindahl, ex-chief executive of ABB, the global technology group, as special advisor on the UN Global Compact. The joining together of the corporate world and the United Nations in order to promote corporate social responsibility is a significant stride and will be conducive to gaining corporate support for the these principles.

Box 3. Voluntary Guidelines for Action on CSR Communication and Reporting

Aimed at European companies, the Voluntary Guidelines were developed on the invitation and with the support of the European Commission. As an increasing number of companies are looking for user-friendly approaches and benchmarking opportunities on how to improve their reporting practices, CSR Europe presented these guidelines, with a specifically business-to business approach in November 2000 at the European Business Convention. They are based on evidence from current business practices of 45 European companies:

- The Voluntary Guidelines encourage companies to undertake Voluntary Reporting on their social and environmental performance across all company operations and make their findings available to stakeholders.

- The Guidelines highlight the use of a variety of communication means to effectively address stakeholders' needs and expectations. These include standards and labels, codes of conduct, web-sites, internal communication, stakeholder consultation, and more.

- They identify a four-step approach to reporting which comprises an in-depth analysis of Processes and Performance on CSR. They encourage companies to report on how they are embedding CSR practices into their core management operations and strategies.

The success of the Voluntary Guidelines will rest in their ability to catalyse bridging between companies' corporate communication and financial assessment by socially responsible investors. The company performance indicators featured in the Guidelines will be further tested and benchmarked against the indicators used by financial analysts to assess company performance on environmental, economic and social issues.

The Lisbon Summit

An extended social security system in Europe since the end of World War II had fostered the view that social cohesion was the business of the state. Whereas in the US social responsibility is rooted in long philanthropic tradition and CSR happens mainly because government does not occupy a very large role, the economic fundamentals today are now such that government on its own cannot fulfil its social obligations in Europe either. This idea was accentuated by the Lisbon Summit of the European Union 23-24 March 2000, where there was recognition of business to assist with the social agenda. This was a historic event as it was the first time that European heads of state and government acknowledged the role of business in this area, and made a formal appeal to business to share its best practices and innovations on social issues. The European Union established a new strategic goal for the next decade: to become the most competitive and dynamic knowledge-based economy in the world, capable of sustainable economic growth with more and better jobs and greater social cohesion. Also stated was the notion of co-ordinating activities in this area amongst Member states, fostering the exchange of experiences and information between the 15 Members, and avoiding duplication.

Following the Lisbon Summit, at the European Council in Feira in June 2000, the appeal to business was reiterated and the initiation of a process to establish a network for a European dialogue on encouraging companies' corporate sense of social responsibility was eagerly accepted. In the Social Policy Agenda adopted there, the Commission stressed the importance of Corporate Social Responsibility in terms of the employment and social consequences of economic and market integration and the adaptation of working conditions in the new economy. Before the end of 2001, the Commission will be issuing a communication supporting initiatives related to CSR and the management of change.

Box 4. The Lisbon Summit of 23-24 March confirmed the commitment to a new economic and social agenda for the European Union

The Heads of State and Government agreed on a new strategic goal for the EU for the next decade: to become the most competitive and dynamic knowledge-based economy in the world capable of sustainable economic growth with more and better jobs and greater social cohesion.

At the same time, an overall strategy was agreed that should allow the EU to achieve this goal as a result of:

- Preparing the transition to the knowledge-based economy and society;
- Promoting economic reforms for competitiveness and innovation;
- Modernising the European Social Model by investing in people and combating social exclusion;
- Sustaining a macro-economic policy mix for sustainable growth.

The Lisbon Conclusions put strong emphasis on the modernisation of the European Social Model and on the development of an active welfare state. For the first time ever, the Conclusions give a high profile to social inclusion and the need for Community activity in this area. The focus in the discussions on the New Social Policy Agenda is the promotion of 'quality'. It is the driving force for a performing economy, more and better jobs and an inclusive society.

Business practices

When examining the issue of CSR in today's global market, one of the most notable features is the shift from the shareholders to the stakeholders, with the stakeholders representing the broader community. CSR is the business sector's response to the non-financial pressures it faces. While critics may disagree about the real motives behind CSR initiatives, seeing them as public relations initiatives by the business community, the speakers at this conference view them as a step towards global convergence of business practices. Alan Christie of Levi-Strauss believes that corporations have a commitment to put something back into the community. This sort of social investment is a chance for a corporation to take a leadership role, making the commitment to run their business in an ethically social and environmental manner. Translating ethical standards into an explicit corporate code is a useful way to communicate that the corporation stands for something.

Companies are taking a more strategic approach in their CSR efforts and significant research and preparation goes into the planning of CSR strategies, determining where a company can make the most effective impact. The role taken on by business, in partnership with the third sector has been a key issue in CSR. Corporations seek strategic involvement in the community in order to address social issues. These issues are chosen by the corporations in order to protect its interests and to enhance its reputation, but at the same time these corporations are investing in response to the needs and appeals of charitable and community organisations. This is done increasingly through partnerships, and corporations rely on the expertise of the third sector in these matters. Fondation de France has 30 years of experience in social projects and is in a position to advise corporations that would like to take action for the public good. With the co-operation of Fondation de France, corporations can invest in regions and distressed areas with the understanding that charity alone is not enough and charity does not make a corporation socially responsible. It is not enough to build a school or a hospital, but companies need to collaborate with the public sector and the community to develop efficient and durable plans. As opposed to pure philanthropy, strategic philanthropy is planned on the long-term with the primary goal being to use the money to make a positive difference, whether this is by fighting exclusion, engaging in a local action in the community, or assisting workers and stakeholders. Providing funds may be necessary, but company commitment should be part of the investment.

PricewaterhouseCoopers in the US has created a division that specifically helps companies with their CSR policies and Business for Social Responsibility has a web-site (www.bsr.org) with substantial research on CSR and offers assistance in planning CSR strategies to their member businesses. In the US, the practice of companies donating for the public good dates back to the 1860s[1], but the trend is increasing in Europe. The fact that CSR has now appeared in the conclusions of two European Union Summits confirms that awareness of this issue in Europe is making a great headway. Working in collaboration with the European Union, CSR Europe (www.csreurope.org) is a business to business network for CSR, with its main objective being to help companies achieve profitability, sustainable growth and human progress. Another European organisation, Business in the Community, is based in the United Kingdom, but is also active in the European agenda. Business in the Community has a core membership of 700 companies that are committed to developing business excellence, engaging companies to focus on key social issues and maximising business resources for the betterment of the local community.

All of the speakers agree that despite the trends of donating intelligently and investing in social causes, there is no substitute for good business practices. Therefore, what really matters is how a company runs its business, its responsibilities to the internal stakeholders, and the values and commitments it places on the corporate codes and the guidelines that we have mentioned. Much of this is embodied within the ILO Declaration on Fundamental Principles and Rights at Work.

The principles concerning the fundamental rights were declared at the International Labour Conference in Geneva, June 1998. They include:

- freedom of association and the effective recognition of the right to collective bargaining;

- the elimination of all forms of forced or compulsory labour;

- the effective abolition of child labour;

- the elimination of discrimination in respect of employment and occupation.

Problems concerning workers' rights, transfer of wealth and equity cannot be overlooked and initiatives taken by the corporations have promoted an accumulation of management expertise that translates ethical notions into the daily operations of a company. Pressures, both internal (from employees) and external (from law, codes, and public opinion) are incorporated into concrete business practice. Thus, CSR is intrinsic to how a company does business and its social responsibility should be essential to all value-based business practice. Values and beliefs become real only when they are lived everyday. No amount of corporate rhetoric or promotion can substitute for direct evidence of a corporation's sincere and meaningful dedication to a consistent set of values that translate into routine behaviour. A genuine socially responsible corporation will set and achieve social and environmental standards even more rigid than what is required by law.

According to a 1995 report released by Ernst & Young's Center for Business Innovation (commissioned by the US Department of Labor), companies that invest in innovative workplace practices are more profitable than those that do not. Investment in environmental controls, community development, worker training and coaching, customer service and responsible citizenship will buy consumer loyalty in years to come.

> '*You can't have the biggest force in society, business, concerned only with maximising profits and still have a socially responsible society.*'[2]
>
> Ben Cohen, of Ben & Jerry's

People are the driving force behind this movement and they must be able to work and live with the changes taking place. Empowerment to the people, those in the community at large and those working for the company should be encouraged by corporations. Corporations are at the heart of the economic life of a community and have a key role to play in development and cohesion in society. It is difficult though to separate the effectiveness of actions taken by corporations from that of the social, political and legal context in which they develop and all sectors need to be functioning coherently together for any progress to be made. Through grant giving, promoting volunteering, and engaging in cause-related marketing, a company can act as a catalyst for change in communities. Managing relations with different groups in civil society and clients for voluntary initiatives enhances the image and the reputation of a corporation. The real challenge for a corporation is to adhere to socially responsible strategies, while at the same time upholding their commitments to shareholders and maintaining turnover.

Conclusions

Business finds itself in a process of evolution, and is changing practices and behaviour to meet the new expectations of communities and society on it. While technological and competitive forces will continue to force companies to be globally integrated, governmental and consumer demands are requiring them to be much more responsive in the social arena, and behaving as a socially responsible corporation is becoming increasingly demanding on companies. They need to contend with the complexities of adhering to social responsibilities in their domestic base as well as in overseas markets, and increased public interest effects the way in which companies promote their initiatives. Policies that demand that a company uphold certain politically correct ideals, such as hiring a certain percentage of minorities or buying goods from a specific source, may at times be undermining to its profitability and product quality. Traditionally profit-seeking managers with challenging quarterly performance targets to meet must also face the challenge of responding to the community needs. Deciding on which approach to take is unique to each company and depends on the business sector in which the company is located, its management structure, its outputs, and its stakeholders. Redefining management roles and relationships in the company itself is not a choice, but a necessity. Companies will need to adapt and create a new organisational model for the 21st century. They need to maximise their effectiveness in decision-making, and make use of internal benchmarking, transfer of best practice, and clear governance processes throughout their organisation.

Socially responsible companies should engage their employees worldwide in a corporate vision and mission statement that promotes sustainable growth and improved quality of life for all countries, for all employees, regardless of their location. Becoming a global leader increases credibility and trust and the notion of a sound business case is a win-win solution that is socially viable and not just a public relations issue. Companies are embracing the challenge of making as much as a positive impact as possible and should be supported by other sectors of society. Thus, although CSR is considered to be a business led initiative, cutbacks made by government in both the US and Europe contributed to creating this new role for business and government still must be involved. Governments need to create a policy framework whereby business and labour can bargain collectively to improve conditions in a company. This requires a range of legislative mechanisms to be implemented at the national, regional, local and multilateral levels. Public policy should be developed encouraging partnerships, voluntary approaches, and market incentives. Governments, along with NGOs, can contribute to raising consciousness and visibility on this issue and help in identifying the best models and procedures for CSR, widening the scope, and facilitating the enactment of initiatives. By working together in co-operation, government, NGOS, and trade unions can monitor corporate behaviour and ensure that certain minimum criteria be upheld.

Companies have in fact made great strides over the last five years, but despite the rising trend for social investment, there is no overall rating system as of yet that incorporates the social notion. Alan Christie and Roy Jones both stated that creating more guidelines is not a workable solution, and even if some companies do in fact have indicators in place, there is a need to focus on what is being benchmarked and to have accountability. It is clear that there cannot be a 'one size fits all' approach to commitment in business conduct, but there is a general agreement that there is a need for clarity of guidelines and standards. In addition to the codes of conduct previously mentioned, an agreed methodology certainly needs to be established in this area so that social action schemes can be developed and social reporting should become the norm. Developing best practices for corporate conduct will not happen immediately, but by adhering to basic principles, all companies would at least move in the same positive direction towards becoming a responsible social partner. Building trust takes time and it is accomplished through consistent, transparent behaviour.

NOTES

1. The beneficiaries of the earliest strategic philanthropy was the Young Men's Christian Association (YMCA) and the benefactors were America's railroad barons. Due to the need for inexpensive housing for their railroad crews, the barons saw the benefit of serving the community and their business at the same time.

2. Cited in *Making Money while Making a Difference -- how to profit with a non-profit partner*, 1999.

PRESENTATIONS BY SPEAKERS

OF THE FIRST PART OF THE ROUNDTABLE DISCUSSIONS

CORPORATE SOCIAL RESPONSIBILITY

IN A GLOBAL ECONOMY

Philanthropy and Social Investment: the French Perspective

Francis Charhon, Director General, Fondation de France

The Fondation de France was created for charitable philanthropy in France 30 years ago and is active in all public interest fields in order to respond to the needs of society, promoting exchanges of expertise in sectors where innovative experiments are now unfolding. We have all heard quite a bit about philanthropy as of late often in very broad terms and Fondation de France recently established the Observatoire de mécenat et générosité (The Study Centre for Philanthropy and Generosity) and analysis of the results of this study will be posted on Internet (site: http://www.fdf.org)

Different approaches of giving in France

There is a strong emergence in Europe of charity giving, and a progression of grants and charity from private citizens and employees. This is mostly due to the modification of behaviour of enterprises towards the environment, and modifications in communication techniques. A recent study of 44 heads of enterprises was undertaken to determine how they see their role in upcoming years. The result was that, in contrast to the early 1990's in France, people are seeing things more positively and see legitimate reasons to get involved in the field of social intervention. With the role of the state is dispersing, local communities and governments are seeking out new partnerships with the private sector.

The concept of a socially responsible corporation is a relatively new concept in France. In the 1990's, the idea evolved of corporate citizenship, of which I do not completely like, because I do not see the corporation as an individual, but an embodiment of several factors. The terminology, corporate social responsibility, is an Anglo-Saxon or American term for Corporate Citizenship or social involvement of the corporation. In France, a multitude of terms are used, such as patronage, sponsoring, partnerships, philanthropy, ethical actions, and particular attention of the differences between these concepts is very important. There are traditional divisions and more modern divisions, with a scale going from sponsoring to philanthropy, with an imaginary cursor that moves according to the level of commitment of a corporation, whether the focus be more on market interests, more on generosity, or, often something in the middle.

The traditional approach is a two-tiered system and the first tier focuses on market value, revenues to shareholders for example. The second tier supports actions here or there, but without a clearly defined general policy for the enterprise, as it is not considered to be very significant or have that much importance.

The new modern approach exists in other countries already and has is a system that is not focused uniquely on production. On the first level, there is a genuine strategic policy, encompassing more than charitable actions. This basic level consists of putting a value chain into place concerning the tools of production, the effects on the environment, child labour, or genetically modified organisms. The second level in this approach concerns the commitment of the corporation towards its entourage. Benefits for those surrounding the enterprise such as job creation, local benefits, improvement of living standards, and quality of life. There is a shift from the shareholders to the stakeholders, with the latter circle being much broader.

The third level of engagement can be most closely linked to the traditional charity system, focusing on local investments, training of local actors, participation in development initiatives for citizens and relationships with NGOs. Despite the link, these policies do not fall in line with traditional ideas of charity. They are more oriented towards a win-win attitude, as described by heads of corporations, '*if my environment is harmonious and satisfying, the image of my company will be good, and the consumer will buy my products.*' This can be seen as cynical, but we cannot overlook the fact that there exists a certain number of heads of enterprises that really do take their social investments very seriously, and they know that they must confront the attitudes of the consumers as well.

Social investment: changing attitudes

The social investments made by corporations, then, are they purely voluntary? The answer is most of the time they are not, for several reasons: due to new methods of communication information about a product or an action of can be transmitted into catastrophic news flash immediately. This has been witnessed in the petroleum industry with the incident of the accident of the Erika in France, and with various issues involving foodstuffs and cosmetics.

I would also like to mention pension funds. Pension funds use an allowance system, and as social investment becomes a factor in the corporation, it becomes an important value for the pension funds as well.

What are the methods of social investment for a corporation? Firstly, there is a strategic plan, and internal acceptance on the part of the board members, shareholders and employees, encompassed in a long-term corporate strategy. Even if in multi-national corporations, policy decisions are made amongst chief board members, the application of these policies are made at the local level, thus we have global and local initiatives functioning together, in order to maintain relations with local collectivities. Examples of this can be seen with the Ronald McDonald House initiatives for terminally ill children taken up by McDonald's, and Johnson and Johnson on health related issues, which are global, but applied locally through each individual country.

As for aid, the idea of simple donations where a check is delivered in response to various solicitors is still taking place, but it has become increasingly difficult for corporations to manage. Thus today, strategy is put into place to clearly define charity giving and is often managed by a corporate communications department. We can see examples of this process in the LVMH corporation, and well as in the development of 'Club d'Entreprises', where enterprises and associations with common interests, join together to form complementary projects. An example of this in France is the 'Club des Partenariats de Culture de l'Hôpital'.

The idea of a Corporate Foundation is quickly developing in France, especially following the passing of the Law 91. This allows for enterprises to display a mainline of development and to maintain a long-term outlook. It contributes to the image of the enterprise, but remains independent as well.

To give some figures on charity and giving in France, culture ranks first. In the last 5 years, social preoccupation has increased, as well as environmental concerns. The volume of investment of 350 million per years in France by corporations is not an extraordinary figure as compared to the United States, but it is an improvement here.

The development of grant giving in terms of goods and services, material, people and competencies, the use of employees towards causes supported by the corporation -- all of this demonstrates how France is changing its attitude towards giving and how the barriers are coming down.

Conclusion

In conclusion, concretely we can note the professionalism of actors, NGOs, intermediary groups (example: Fondation de France), and the creation on international networks, like the European Centre for Foundations, allowing for shared knowledge and the ability to work together on some issues as social capital.

The fiscal environment is also very important, as a corporation will not be apt to make social investments if the fiscal system is too complicated. This can be especially true for SMEs, smaller and modest enterprises, even more than MNEs who can perhaps invest in social actions, but need a simply fiscal system in order to do so.

Of course the factors behind all of this can be found in the ethics and the values of the corporation. How can a corporation decide what is good for the public, as they have neither the authority nor the right to be the agent of general public interest? Therefore, it is fundamental to look at their behaviour and establish codes of conduct so that partnerships may be made amongst the various actors that work on social actions and develop social action schemes.

The Role of Business in the Social Agenda

Alan Christie, CSR Europe,
Vice President , Public Affairs, Levi Strauss Europe, Middle East, & Africa, and Chairman of the Board of Directors, CSR Europe

The corporate view

My comments will waver between the approach of Françis Charhon and Donald Johnston. I want to speak about the context in which CSR takes place. From the point of view of a corporation, it is inevitable that we ask what is good for business? Our business and business in general. What's the impact on the corporation? I do think that in fact companies are like individuals as they have individual characteristics and individual philosophies of business and individual needs with respect to market places. In regards to Levi Strauss, I want to give some examples from that point of view, but I am also wearing my other hat as chairman of the board of directors of the European Business Network for Social Cohesion (EBNSC), now newly named CSR Europe, and speak generally about business as a whole.

The Levi Strauss philosophy

Levi Strauss has an advantage because it is a privately held company held by the same family for 140 years, and today have evolved and maintained their philosophy of how to do business. The company has a core set of values that puts emphasis on its relationship with the community and its stakeholders. Levi-Strauss has a commitment to put something back into the community, broadly defined. To illustrate that, four areas of activity with broad and general relevance can be mentioned:

Philanthropy

François Charhon spoke of social investment, or philanthropy of charities, but the process of corporations putting something back into the community is an old and voluntary process. There has been a change, and that change is that companies recognise the opportunity to be active and be seen to be active, to take a leadership role to make things change and to make things happen through philanthropic activities. In our case at Levi-Strauss, the most important initiative was a decision in the early 1980s to support HIV and Aids initiatives, a disease that at the time was regarded with horror by the community at large. It took some courage for a corporation not directly involved in the treatment and management of that disease to decide it wanted to be publicly identified to this epidemic. So, philanthropy as a mechanism bearing wealth or creating resources is an opportunity for companies to demonstrate leadership.

Employee relations

Obviously, the relationship between a company and its employees is one of the most fundamental ways in which a company can demonstrate its social responsibility. I don't think it is possible for a company to claim social responsibility through charitable giving on one hand and being a poor employer on the other. It is a holistic concept and all aspects have to be right. There will be endless arguments about what constitutes a good employer. I am more than conscious that the retail industry is traditionally known for low pay for the majority of its workers, but I would contend that we have a long-standing commitment and practice of good behaviour of excellence in the conduct of our employee relations.

I can count endless examples of how that has manifested itself. Starting with the San Francisco, California earthquake of 1906, where despite being wiped out like every other business in the city, we nevertheless kept and maintained our workforce. During the depression of the 1930's in the United States, we maintained our workforce once again through 'make-work projects' to keep people employed. In recent years when changes in the business world has required restructuring and reducing our manufacturing capacity, I think we, in co-operation with various trade unions, managed to put together severance and exit strategies that were exemplary in their particular region or country, and particularly in this industry. Therefore, commitment to employees is a fundamental characteristic to any commitment to corporate social responsibility.

Diversity

We have also played a role in commitment to diversity regarding globalisation, which we see as the movement of people and ideas around the globe, the creation of a much more multi-ethnic and multi-cultural world than has traditionally been the case. It does seem to me that companies are in many ways social microcosms in the community in which they exist, and they have a particular role to play in recognising values and driving that process toward multi-culturism and multi-ethnicism. It is certainly a process that our company has supported.

In the 1960s in the Southern United States, we were one of the first companies to desegregate our factories. This was done despite huge local resistance, including problems from those people with white sheets and pointy hats* who made life rather difficult for our managers in that part of the world. In the 1990's in the United States, we launched 'Project Change' designed to bring communities together across the ethnic divide at a time when ethnic tension was rising and a lot of people in the US did not want to deal with it. Strangely enough, the same people in the sheets and pointy hats were making our work difficult once again. Nevertheless, this demonstration of leadership in corporate social responsibility was very important for us to drive change.

Relations with developing countries

The last area I will mention is the area of sourcing, especially sourcing a product from outside the countries where key markets are, in other words, from developing countries. We were the first major multi-national corporations to publish a code of conduct to govern in an ethical way our business relationships with our contractors in developing countries in 1991. At that time, we were referred to as *weirdoes*. There was not a lot of public demand for codes from either activist groups, trade unions or governments for companies to adopt practices of that kind. Things have certainly changed quite a bit, since today it seems as if everyone in the world has an opinion of how a code of conduct should be written and how it should be monitored and implanted, and that is fine and appropriate. The recent revision of the OECD Guidelines for Multi-National Corporations was welcome by our company and we engaged enthusiastically in the debate, as there was nothing in those guidelines that we had to worry about or that any company should be worried about. These guidelines are a logical, rational, and appropriate basis in order to conduct business.

---

* Reference to the Klu Klux Klan.

Corporations against social exclusion

In the course of the last 10 years, we have switched from being labelled a slightly eccentric, west coast, hippie, *weirdo-type* company to being much closer to the mainstream, and this is not because we have changed, but because the business climate has changed and changed rather significantly. The chairman mentioned CSR Europe, which I have the privilege of chairing at the moment. This was created in 1995, upon a challenge that was laid down in front of European businesses by the President Delors before he left office. It came about as the result of conversations and conferences that had taken place following the European Declaration of Business Against Social Exclusion in Brussels at that time. The message was simply: the rise of social exclusion and the rise of the underclass has become perhaps the biggest challenge facing the political establishment today. What is the business community going to do to contribute to finding a response to this challenge? In the beginning, a lot of businesses looked around slightly bedazzled thinking, '*What does this have to do with us?*' '*What should we do about something like this?*'. Now 5 years later, a lot has changed. Just last week in Brussels, we had a conference with 450 people, the vast majority from the European business community. There was a parallel conference in New York, a similar organisation called, Business for Social Responsibility (http://www.bsr.org), with 800 people, primarily from business. We have come a long way in 5 years, to a point where business mainstream understands the need to engage in the issue of CSR.

Facing globalisation

CSR is no longer the providence of a select few. At the outcome of the Lisbon Summit amongst heads of government, there was an explicit recognition of the role of business to contribute and assist with the social agenda. I think it was an incredibly important step and will be the base of discussions over the next 5 years. Why did it all happen? What happened to Milton Friedman's 'business of business is business' mantra? We all remember the move in the 1980's towards smaller government, lower taxes, less regulation, more privatisation of public service. With the fall of the communist system in the end of the 1980's, we saw that the free market was the only game in town. If solutions are to be found for social problems, they need to be found in the context of the free market and of course, business plays a rather large part in the functioning of the free market.

The focus of attention falls on the business community in the search for solutions and today even more so due to globalisation. Globalisation is good for business, it has increased our options, increased our mobility, both in terms of our sourcing opportunities and our market. It has also increased access to information, it has made more people more involved, more aware, more convinced that they have a role to play and that has inevitably increased pressure on businesses, making the need for transparency in business activities all the more apparent. It is a challenge that government faces and perhaps the reason why government seeks an alliance with business as we are all more and more in search of solutions to these many difficult problems.

Meeting expectations

Business finds itself in a process of evolution. We are changing practices and behaviour to meet the new expectations of communities and society on us. This is reflected by many different forces, whether it is governmental or non-governmental, expectations of business behaviour and the role of business has changed dramatically and I suspect will continue to change. What seems correct and appropriate today, a generation from now will seem practically Keynesian. The fact that most of us work 5 days a week and take 3 weeks of holiday a year is going to seem barbaric 20-30 years from now, as when we look at the working conditions of the early part of the 20th century, they appear barbaric from our prospective.

Through this process of evolution, we are attempting to meet the expectations that society place upon us and I think that business is increasingly willing and open to take up those challenges. It will take time, progress is uneven, of that there can be no doubt, and there will be a 2 step forward, 3 step back, and 2 step to the side process along the way. I do however, think that there will be a trend, a tendency which is inevitable and is heading in a broadly specific direction. I think it will be true to say that the majority of companies, particularly the larger MNCs are now on board.

I am not going to make any commitments to the companies other than my own, but I do believe that we are in a situation today where there is a much more receptive environment for dialogue between business and those who question the roles and the behaviour of business. The challenge for all of us is to find ways to encourage, enhance and deepen that dialogue, and on that basis I think we will be able to move forward.

Internal Stakeholders and High Road Companies

Roy Jones, Senior Policy Advisor,
Trade Union Advisory Committee to the OECD

To discuss what makes a company socially responsible it is important to identify the values and commitments it must implement. Equally important is to identify the processes by which to achieve that. My comments will focus on the values and commitments as they relate to a company's internal practices, particularly those relating to workers. I know that other speakers will discuss how company practices impact on the external environment, for example the wider community.

For trade unions the values and commitments in question are embodied within the ILO Declaration on Fundamental Principles and Rights at Work. These are: freedom of association and the effective recognition of the right to collective bargaining; the elimination of all forms of forced or compulsory labour; the effective abolition of child labour; and the elimination of discrimination in respect of employment and occupation. Optimum levels of training or other employment practices flow from these core labour standards. We cannot talk about corporate social responsibility without ensuring the implementation of these enabling rights.

The '*Partners for Progress -- Towards a New Approach to corporate social responsibility*', corresponds to what we at the Trade Union Advisory Committee to the OECD (TUAC) see as the way to embed these values and commitments in corporate practices, namely 'partnerships' between business and organised labour. It may well be fashionable to include the word 'new' in conference titles, but it's worth reminding ourselves that the 'old' approaches are still the best approaches, where the representatives of workers and business sit down together to work out an agreement.

Corporate social responsibility -- to whom -- shareholders or stakeholders?

To discuss the ends and the means of corporate social responsibility we need a conceptual framework. Today, there are two competing models: the shareholder value model, where corporations exist only to maximise financial returns to shareholders; and the stakeholder model, where shareholders join others, such as workers and management in having some claim to a say in how a company is run, and to its residual profits. External stakeholders also exist, including suppliers, creditors, and wider communities. Each has different roles and responsibilities, which require different mechanisms to allow them to be exercised.

The real world of 'high and low road' companies

There is no doubt that in the real world there exist many good companies that practice social responsibility -- let's call them 'high road' corporations. But the fact that we are having this debate reflects the reality that there exists too many companies that are not socially responsible -- let's call them 'low road' corporations. The danger in all of this is that the latter come to dominate the former. The reasons for this are outside the scope of this presentation, save to say that they lie in the lack of an effective policy response by governments to the political and economic challenges of the post-cold war order, and globalisation, and their impact on developing and developed countries alike.

That brings in a key dimension to this debate: market forces acting outside of a regulated policy framework set by governments will only deliver marginal improvements in corporate social responsibility. Furthermore, governments cannot privatise their responsibilities to companies and markets unless they are willing to accept the inevitable political backlash. Rather, what we need are economic and social policies that help create long-term economically, socially and environmentally sustainable firms -- our 'high road' companies. These firms recognise trade unions and bargain with them in good faith; invest in physical and human capital; and grow organically, rather than simply by mergers and acquisitions. The company's profits are redistributed equitably between internal stakeholders, owners, managers and workers, and the company has a comfortable relationship in the community in which it is located. By contrast 'low-road' firms are short-termist as regards investment in physical and human capital; adopt a conflictual attitude to trade unions and other workers' rights; and grow through aggressive mergers and acquisitions. Major and growing problems exist around the internal distribution of wealth, for example through executive remuneration packages that in effect transfer (steal?) money from both shareholders and workers, while bearing no relation to any measure of company performance.

This leads to the question of whether it is 'high' or 'low road' corporations that predominate. The answer varies across countries and across sectors. Many large companies, especially multinationals are joining the corporate social responsibility movement – witness the explosion in corporate codes of conduct. Some of these are doing it for cynical reasons – in an attempt to protect their brand image. Some are doing it because they understand that they must take responsibility for the behaviour of their subsidiaries and suppliers. Hopefully those with genuine intentions will prevail, but at the moment the jury is out, especially regarding the role of codes.

Insecurity in the workplace

Let me cite a few examples. A recent Cornell University study for the US Deficit Review Commission (*Uneasy Terrain: The Impact of Capital Mobility on Workers, Wages, and Union Organising)* found that despite the longest boom in history, workers in America are feeling more insecure than they have ever felt before. More than half of the employers surveyed had threatened to close either all or part of a plant during trade union organising drives. In some sectors that figure rose to 68 per cent, and was always unrelated to the financial conditions of a company. That threat provokes a great sense of insecurity making it is very difficult for workers to gain better standards of living. Around 10 000 US workers per year are illegally sacked for trying to organise a union. Other US research shows that when workers lose jobs, the likelihood is that the next one will have lower wages, decreased health benefits and lower pension entitlements. As a previous speaker said, '*What is good for business?*' My response would be not that strategy. And it also puts into perspective the claims of some claiming to act in a socially responsible way.

This behaviour spreads far beyond the US shores. TUAC surveys its affiliates every 4 years on what is happening in multinational corporations. The situation regarding employment practices is in many instances deteriorating. None more so than the use by management of threats to close or re-locate the plant as a weapon to influence collective bargaining. In developing countries it is often worse, partly due to heightened competition for international investment between developing countries, and within that the exponential growth of export processing zones, outsourcing and lengthening supply chains, with little social accountability. In China for example, there are over 1000 exporting processing zones covering vast geographical areas where human rights are systematically abused.

As for external stakeholders, the United States Institute of Taxation and Economic Policy has recently studied the tax paying habits of 250 publicly traded companies. Over 10 per cent did not pay taxes in 1998, a third paid taxes at less than 50 per cent of the official rate of corporate tax, and 12 corporations with over $12.2 billion in profits were found to have received $535 million in tax credits.

Ensuring corporate social responsibility

All of this begs the question. What is to be done? Some would argue that governments should leave corporate social responsibility to individual companies. It is precisely that hands off policy that has spawned an industry of conferences on this subject, as opposed to improving workplace standards. That policy has also fed the backlash against corporations.

Rather, what is needed is for governments to create a policy framework whereby business and labour can bargain collectively to improve conditions in a company. It may be old fashioned to some, but that still remains the best way to ensure corporate social responsibility. That will require a range of hard and soft law mechanisms to be implemented at the national, regional, and multilateral levels.

Leaving aside future or existing hard mechanisms, such as a workers' rights clause in international trade and investment agreements, or European social legislation, a tool kit of soft law mechanisms is emerging that could help to attain our goal. The OECD Guidelines for Multinational Enterprises have now been revised to include a government backed implementation mechanism. I would urge companies to publicly adhere to the Guidelines, and to sit down with the relevant trade union body to ensure their implementation. The UN Global Compact is another tool that aims to create a dialogue and a process of engagement between business and labour. That too has a role to play in achieving our aims.

The role of trade unions

Trade unions though are not just waiting for governments. Outside of the plethora of national level agreements, there now exists around ten 'framework agreements' negotiated between International Trade Secretariats (representing sectoral unions such as metal workers) and multinational enterprises. These are about establishing a relationship between multinationals and unions. Corporate codes of conduct exist too, but it is important to distinguish between what is in effect a pledge to the public by a company concerning its behaviour or that of its suppliers, and the OECD Guidelines or a framework agreement. That is not to decry codes. Over time some of them may develop into useful parts of the tool kit, for example SA8000. But much remains to be done to ensure that they move beyond being a public pledge to deliver corporate social responsibility, into something that guarantees it.

The reality remains however, that we can have as many hard or soft laws and regulations as we can draft, but they will remain fine words outside of any meaningful compliance by corporations. For that to happen a reversal of the prevailing mindset is required among governments and corporations, whereby the de-regulation and liberalisation mantra gives way to a serious debate around the type of architecture needed to govern globalisation, and the regulatory foundations needed to support it. And, on the policy front, the inter-governmental organisation that best responds, and sets out a credible agenda to meet that challenge will reap the rewards. Similarly, those corporations that recognise that they will gain by being part of the team will gain too. Trade unions at all levels are ready to play their part in this. The question remains – are employers ready, willing and able to join us?

Making a Positive Impact on Society

Chris Marsden, Senior Visiting Fellow, Corporate Citizenship Unit, Warwick Business School

What companies should be doing

What makes a company socially responsible? I think that this question can be interpreted in two ways. Firstly, what would a company have to be doing make it socially responsible. Secondly, what are the driving forces that make a company behave in a socially responsible way? They are both important questions. For those of us trying to promote corporate social responsibility, the first question is about defining our objective -- what we want companies to be doing -- and the second concerns how we might achieve it -- how companies can be persuaded to be socially responsible. I have only time to address the first question here right now, but hope that the second will be taken up in the discussion session, as it is the key policy question.

What would a socially responsible company be doing to deserve such a title? It is certainly not just one that gives a lot of money to charity. Pure charity -- in other words, disinterested giving -- is, in my opinion, for individuals not for companies, especially public shareholder-owned companies. Disinterested giving cannot easily be justified to shareholders. Nor is a socially responsible company necessarily one that invests a good percentage of its profits in community programmes. This is self-interested giving, if you like. It may be enlightened self-interest based on a company's need to operate in a thriving society. It may be designed to foster relationships, build reputation, enhance staff morale or even promote the brand. This is all entirely legitimate, business-justified activity and may do a great deal of good both to the community and the company, but it does not create a socially responsible company in itself. It may indeed be part of what a socially responsible company does but it can never be enough on its own.

Corporate community investment is only a tiny part of the overall impact of the company -- say, a 1/2, 1 or even 5% or pre-tax profits amounting to probably less than 0.1% of the value of turnover. Giving away some of your profits can never be a substitute for poor business practices elsewhere -- it is how you earn your profits in the first place that matters most. Community investment can, however, be a very effective entry point for a company's engagement with social issues and provide leverage for involvement of mainstream business operations. But it is how a company carries out its mainstream business operations that determine whether or not it is socially responsible.

Running a good business

Ten years ago it was my job to try to help BP develop an understanding of its social responsibility. At that time the company had a code of ethical practice, was already developing a strong environmental strategy and had a number of good community programmes. However, there was little joined up thinking about its overall responsibility to society, especially regarding social issues, which most managers then regarded as something the company paid taxes to the government to deal with.

I found the following approach, based on Peter Drucker's analysis, a very helpful starting point in management discussions:

Being socially responsible means:

1. running YOUR activity safely, legally and effectively;
2. minimising your adverse impact on community and society (*i.e.*, do no harm);
3. addressing those social issues which:
   a) impact your activity;
   b) are within your competence to influence;
   c) offer opportunities for mutual benefit.

The purpose of this was firstly to show that social responsibility was about the whole of business activity, not just about community investment (which is what many managers assumed it to be) and, secondly, that investment in community programmes should be an integral part of business strategy. It emphasised that the most fundamental part of social responsibility is to run a good business well. If you poll public opinion about the purpose of business, you will tend to get the straightforward and obvious response that it is to provide valued goods and services and to provide jobs -- in other words the means for local people to earn a living. Doing this cost-effectively, profitably, safely and legally is a company's first task.

Its second socially responsible task is to recognise and reduce to a minimum any social or environmental costs it might be inflicting on society. This often implies setting and achieving standards beyond that required by the law. This is a particularly important issue for international companies operating in third world countries.

The third task concerns not just minimising a company's negative impact but making as much as possible of a positive impact. This is a tough one for cost-conscious profit seeking managers with challenging quarterly performance targets to meet. In order to limit this otherwise potentially frightening and open-ended expectation of business involvement in social issues, it is suggested that a company should focus on issues that are:

– relevant to its business and environment;

– can engage its inherent expertise and resources;

– can bring benefits to the company as well as community groups.

A public service commitment

Ten years on, BP, Shell and a number of other companies, like those taking part in this and similar seminars (like the seminar last week organised by EBNSC, CSR Europe today), the converted if you like, would accept this kind of more holistic definition of a socially responsible company. They would say that it is a company which understands, or at least seeks to understand, the effects on society of all its business practices -- positive and negative, actual and potential -- and which integrates the active management of these impacts into the company's central governance and accountability structure -- so that performance in such things is part of managers' quarterly targets.

It is very similar to the concept of the 'public service' commitment that typically governments impose on privatised utilities. Whereas this tends to be focused on provision of their product (water, electricity, telephones, etc.) to poor communities, the idea of a 'public service' contribution of a company can easily be extended to its practices regarding employment and procurement, health, safety, ethical trading and impacts on the social and ecological environment. They are the outputs of a company. Corporate social responsibility, then, is voluntary acceptance by a company of a kind of public service commitment to manage effectively such 'outputs' of their business.

Ten years ago many of these companies, and certainly BP, might have had a strategy of 'let alone and hope such issues never bother us'. Perhaps they backed up this 'ignore and hope' strategy with some kind of emergency response procedure planned in case of a crisis and some basic management codes of practice and compliance assurance procedures as a potential legal defence if things did go wrong. Today a socially responsible company will anticipate and manage such issues as they arise, backed up by a well thought-through vision and policy statement, a code of ethical practice, clear governance processes throughout the entire organisation, internal and external accountability, reporting and auditing, risk analysis, stakeholder dialogue processes and staff training. Some are even going further and taking a leadership role by building partnerships with stakeholders and actively engaging in issues beyond their immediate impact on the company in order to influence the development of the issue itself. BP and Shell are doing this with global warming, Levi Strauss with responsible sourcing in Third World countries and The Body Shop with animal testing are all examples of such companies. I am not suggesting that these companies are model corporate citizens. I don't know of any such thing. But they, and a number of others like them, have made clear, public commitments to run their businesses in an ethically, socially and environmentally responsible way and through their increasingly transparent and stakeholder-engaging accountability processes are demonstrating a genuine will to improve. They have a long way to go in many cases. That is certainly the foundation for making a socially responsible company.

The effects of globalisation

CSR becomes increasingly important due to globalisation. This active engagement approach to issue management is particularly important for big trans-national companies operating in global markets with global networking technology. The absence of effective global governance is creating an imperative for active engagement by companies in social and environmental issues. This point was strongly made in the 1999 UNCTAD World Investment Report:

> *'Economic models that rely on competitive market disciplines and the regulatory functioning of public authorities do not fully capture the dynamics of the current globalizing economy, particularly for developing countries in which marketplace competition is often insufficiently developed and governmental resources are often inadequate for the task of effective regulation. Under these circumstances, a governance vacuum may develop, underlining the responsibilities of TNCs.'*

Even in countries which appear to have a well-governed business environment and a culture that still maintains a strong public sector ethos, things are rapidly changing. As national governments are increasingly restricted in their freedom to regulate and in their taxing and social spending capabilities by imperatives of global competitiveness, the need for newly liberated enterprise to exercise active social responsibility is increasingly important. Such corporate social responsibility is probably not a long term substitute for properly constituted forms of global governance, whatever they might turn out to be, but it can be a potentially crucial, interim building block towards dealing with the worst deficiencies of the free market, whilst maintaining most of the benefits.

The European Union's Approach to Corporate Social Responsibility

Marie Donnelly, Head of Unit, Adaptation to Industrial Change, European Commission

New challenges for Europe

CSR is not new in Europe. It existed for many years, although perhaps expressed in different ways. But what is certainly true is to say that the concept of CSR received a major impetuous in the Lisbon Summit in March of this year, when heads of government sited the issue in their conclusions covering the challenges faced today. They specified that by 2001, the EU is to be the most dynamic and socially cohesive economy in the world and in achieving those objectives there was a realisation by the heads of government that this could only be built within partnerships. There was a direct appeal made to business in the context of CSR. I think that it was the first time that head of government addressed such an invitation to the business community in the conclusions of such a meeting. How can partnership operate in the context of CSR, especially given that it is a very multi-dimensional area? There are many actors; there are also stakeholders and shareholders. It is impossible to say it is just one or two groups working in collaboration, as there are many groups that have a legitimate role to play. Today I would like to focus on the issue of public-private partnership. The notion of putting together private enterprise and public authority and then viewing some of the ways in which this process can be facilitated, particularly in the view of the public authorities.

The first thing I would like to clarify is that the EC sees CSR as a business led initiative, an issue very similar to quality. In the 1950's, 'quality' was something that was stamped onto a product at the end of the production line. Today, nobody believes that you can add quality to a product at the end of the process. Quality is intrinsic and design, selection of ingredients, delivery, after-care service, and destroying the product or the packaging after its use, demonstrate that clearly, quality is instringent and likewise, in an analogous way, CSR is also intrinsic to the way companies do business. It cannot be added in, it cannot be imported from the outside, and it cannot be compartmentalised into another area of activity. However, we do believe that public authorities have an important role to play in stimulating debate, encouraging, and in some cases, pushing private enterprise to achieve higher standards and to go forward faster than perhaps they had been.

Initiatives of the European Union

Public authorities in Europe have undertaken four areas of activity.

Visibility

The first area covers the question of visibility touching upon the idea of raising awareness and drawing attention to this subject matter. One of our biggest activities in this context is in the political domain. I believe that the fact that CSR as a concept has now appeared in the conclusions of two European summits is already an important initiative and an important awareness raising activity, but it does not end there. There are specific interaction possibilities and the European Union organised a conference on CSR in May of this year and then last week we collaborated very closely with the EBNSC (today called CSR Europe) at the conference in Brussels. In an ongoing sense, this activity of raising awareness and visibility intrinsically means that we would become a forum for dialogue with business and other groups and other stakeholders, including other parts of business, financial institutions, NGO, and consumer groups.

Identify best practice

The second are is to both identify and build on best practice, which is the basis in which the best European model will emerge. We could take the view to deepen understanding of CSR, examine how it operates, as well as the procedures and mechanisms of company reporting. Or, we could say that we should widen the approach in order to have a more important scope of coverage for CSR. For the moment, the EC has opted for the latter option.

The Commission is very concerned about avoiding a situation where we have a divide in Europe, as for example with the information society where we already have a North-South divide. We do not want that to occur in the area of CSR and in terms of deepening the issue, we can benefit from the experts in the field and thus take up the challenge of how we can make CSR attractive and interesting to a whole range of the corporate sector, both big companies and small companies. CSR is not just the domain of large enterprises, this is very relevant to SMEs, and it must be stressed that 90 per cent of the enterprise fabric in Europe consists of SMEs, thus we will never achieve an attitude of CSR in Europe unless we are able to bring SMEs on board in this context.

CSR issues concern to all sectors of the economy and the Commission has supported the Voluntary Guidelines on CSR Communicating that were adopted last week at the EBNSC conference in Brussels. It is a simple document and it is a very deliberate strategy. For those who are experts on the subject matter, you may find the document to be superficial. One of the reasons that this document was put together in collaboration with business was that there are already many initiatives and there is an enormous scope for confusion. It is very important to have a simple message that people can catch on to, and in this context the document is effectively a first attempt to introduce people to what CSR is.

It is built on an approach that there are principles and practices, there is a process and then performance is measured. There are four phases and these phases can be used across a range of issues: the workplace, the market place, the community, environment, ethics and human rights. It is presented in an 'a la carte' manner, so a company may just start with the principles in two or three areas and see how it develops and then gradually extend in relation to particular environment, kind of business, the size of the company, the number of workers, etc. It is a progressive option, but the message is to start and to start this process soon. In that context these guidelines are seen as an important initiative adding support and stimulation to this public-private partnership in CSR.

A sound case for business

The third area of activity is the notion of a sound business case, a win-win solution that is socially viable and not just a public relations issue. In the context of CSR, there is another important actor, and that is the financial institutions. The financial institutions have two roles:

- Firstly, they need to be corporate socially responsible citizens, and thus the proposal to establish a banking services charter, with guaranteed minimal services to be in place for when the Euro currency is launched in January 2002. This is an example of the financial institutions taking responsibility for their role within society.
- Secondly, the support of micro-credits for social activity and very small enterprises is crucial.

Financial institutions cannot just be responsible to themselves; their role goes beyond what they do as corporate entities in the sense that they also drive the whole process of CSR as operators and guardians of socially responsible investment. For this in Europe there is a distinct challenge because at the moment there is not a clear mechanism for identifying socially responsible companies. No measures are in place or indicators agreed upon or operational. In Member states, there are already operations in place and there is already a number of rating agencies with well-developed methodologies determined to meet the local demand. However, we do not have a European approach. It is not to say that we need to replace all existing methodologies in place, but we need to have an agreed methodology that can be used for a European investment market.

There is a gap at the moment, but I am very impressed by the project that was presented at the conference last week in Brussels, where rating agencies in Europe got together and combined their expertise in order to provide an analysis of 45 companies. This shows that it is possible to work together in a common methodology and the EC can facilitate the collaboration between the experts in this area so that from these collaborations we can establish a single methodology that can become the methodology for European based, European wide investments. In this context we can envisage moving toward the direction of having a European social index. I realise that this is not an easy task to achieve, but I believe it can be done, and I would like to say that perhaps we could even have it in place prior to the currency change.

Co-ordination amongst Member states

The fourth area clearly underpins the previous activities. It entails co-ordinating Member states' activities in a given domain. Under the French presidency of the EC, there will be a meeting in December 2000 in Nice to exchange information and experience in CSR with the important intent of avoiding duplication. For example there is a great deal of enthusiasm and action in Member states at the moment and there are initiatives for either a rating index nationally or a social labelling system for either products or companies. Our concern is that if an individual Member state were to develop a social labelling system, the risk exists that it may only be valid for companies of that Member state. This would then place them at an advantage regarding companies operating in other Member states and trying to enter the market. It could also perhaps become a barrier in an internal market, so although it is important that we have individual initiatives, it can lead to contradictions.

Although we firmly believe that CSR is very much the domain of the enterprise, there are very important areas where public authority can facilitate, stimulate and maybe even prod enterprises in a direction that delivers CSR as an intricate part of doing business in Europe.

PART 2

STIMULATING PARTNERSHIPS WITH BUSINESS AT THE LOCAL LEVEL

Overview of discussions

The second part of the roundtable discussions were devoted to the role of firms in the local community and partnerships for tackling social exclusion and other inner city problems. Non-profit organisations play a leading role in this area, but major corporations have much to contribute both in terms of finance but also knowledge and experience. There was broad agreement amongst participants that stimulating partnerships remains the key to solving the problems of exclusion and dealing with the new challenges of globalisation as they are played out at the local level. In overcoming the hurdles of social responsibility, all partners and sectors need to be committed to adhere to a coherent strategy in the interest of society as a whole.

Moreover, small and medium sized enterprises can make substantial contributions to ameliorating the economic and social problems of local communities. Despite the impact that MNCs have on society, small and medium-sized enterprises play a key role in economic and social development and regeneration. The struggle between the forces of global commerce and the interests of local cultures brings with it new politics, and local cultures are a countervailing force to the global economy and a necessary precondition for its continued existence. While the adage 'think globally, act locally', may sound a bit trite, it nevertheless reflects the thinking of third sector organisations worldwide and a growing number of business representatives. The tension between global and local does exist however. Companies are local and global at the same time and there is competition at the local level (city, region) to determine who gains access to contracts and investments. Local SMEs are also becoming global companies; SMEs are entering into international joint ventures, strategic alliances, and franchising, all contributing to development of global partnerships amongst smaller firms and MNCs. E-commerce and technology also help level the playing field and help local SMEs to think globally and interact with foreign partners.

Large corporations and SMEs

Large corporations supporting SMEs

Large companies have a role to play in order to re-enforce a bottom-up approach in the implementation of CSR. These companies can support linkages with small and micro-enterprises through their core business activities, their social investment or philanthropic activities and their influence on the public policy agenda. Multi-national corporations can assist SMEs in a number of ways in their locality. One of the most obvious and beneficial to both the large and the small companies is mentoring. By placing a representative from an MNC into the boardroom of a supplier or on an advisory board of a local technical college, business and staff relations can be improved. Many business leaders from large companies serve as advisors and trustees on boards of micro-finance intermediaries and NGOs, which have been established, to support SME development.

Certain companies encourage their managers to volunteer for such activities. For example, The Prince's Youth Trust in the United Kingdom runs a successful and innovative programme that matches individual mentors, usually business people with a wide range of expertise and young entrepreneurs in order to give them managerial support, business advice and personal encouragement. The international accountancy and management consultancy, KPMG, has a mentoring support programme. They offer support for the professional development of teachers in inner city schools. Managers from KPMG work as mentors with the teachers, meeting with them and providing on-going support and advice on the increasingly complex management issues of running their schools.

Large corporations can also help by providing finance to SMEs. From seed investment to significant equity stakes, MNCs can bring in capital that boost the SME endeavours, either through the supply chain or simply by bolstering their overall quality of the local business community. Helping local companies through the start-up phase and into the growth phase will promote diversity, stability, and better overall business practices within the heart of the local economy. In the United Kingdom for example, the Corporate Responsibility Group (CRG) is a group of 48 leading United Kingdom companies who have expressed commitment to CSR. The members of large companies would like to play a role in supporting and encouraging SMEs to place social and environmental responsibility as an important basis for their business practice.

SMEs need to attract, develop, and retain good staff in order to enter into lucrative international supply chains. Large corporations have the necessary knowledge to assist SMEs with professional training and business organisation. They are experienced in developing and implementing tailored training programmes and can extend these to the local business community. It is a cost-effective way of enhancing skills and good business practice as well as quality ethos. Large companies can also contribute to research and development by offering support on a voluntary basis by establishing university chairs and research programmes to focus on SME development. SMEs can also use facilities of large corporations and use their equipment or supplies.

Although mentoring and financial provision will be helpful at the start-up stage, an already established SME may need a different type of support such as for develop potential or enhancing business skills and standards. Some large companies establish small business units to facilitate SME development. One example of this is Anglo-American and De Beers Small and Medium Enterprise Initiative (SMEI). This self-funding unit was established in 1989 to promote and manage business links between the groups' operating companies and small-scale businesses. It acts as a venture capitalist company, taking minority equity stakes and making loans to SMEs. This unit also established advisory centres located in different towns to identify investment and purchasing options and to offer training, advice, and mentoring to SME partners.

Box 5. Telefonica de Espana: supportive relationships with SMEs

One example of how a large corporation can help the development of small businesses and job creation is that of Telefonica in Spain and one of its 2 000 small suppliers, Inelcom, which produces electronic systems to automate the grading of farm produce. In the early 1980's, Inelcom's small R&D team designed a monitoring system which they then sold to Telefonica. This transaction completely changed the span of Inelcom's activities in the field. Telefonica's trust in Inelcom's capacity to innovate enabled the SME to finance the development of new product designs. With each successful new product, Inelcoms expanded its technological capabilities, broadened its product range and created jobs in R&D, manufacture and installation. Turnover grew to ECU25 million, with exports accounting for 25 per cent.

Entrepreneurship and franchising

Entrepreneurship is a critical element in creating active and powerful market economies and entrepreneurship can be stimulated with the support of large companies to smaller local businesses. This sort of intervention benefits all actors in a locality, contributing to the quality of life in a locality. When companies reach out to schools to teach students about entrepreneurship and the world of business, an entrepreneurial culture may be developed, reducing dependency through building sustainable livelihoods. For the company itself, brand image and reputation are enhanced, contributing to employee recruitment and retention. Good business practices are also developed with other business partners, strengthening the supply-chain and increasing local procurement opportunities. In this context, the government may also contribute to building a sustainable SME sector, thus creating an enterprise friendly business environment and creating employment.

Franchising has become the most important form of business organisation since the advent of the modern corporation at the beginning of the twentieth century. It has spread throughout the world, replacing traditional independently owned single businesses. The area of franchising and leasing is also of growing importance in linkages between MNCs and SMEs, since through franchising, large corporations began creating small businesses to act as local surrogates. In many companies, major oil companies for instance, programmes have been developed to help indigenous entrepreneurs operate services that they either own or lease, while the company provides them with a package of support services, such as administrative or book-keeping training and advice on business management, environmental management, marketing and retailing.

The presence of a franchise upgrades social responsibility in an area. The franchise, with the support of the large company, is able to contribute to their local market and assist the community with more ease than their traditional counterparts. The franchises are obligated to uphold the standards of the larger corporation, regardless of their locality. Whether these standards concern employing workers or distributing goods and services, consumers and employees tend to trust these franchises because of the image of the parent company behind it. In the United States, the franchise is fast becoming the dominant form of local enterprise.

CSR and SMEs

While large companies can offer SMEs advice, professional support and share information, and the flow of knowledge between MNCs and SMEs is a two way street. Most SMEs develop a holistic approach to CSR and do not see it as a corporate strategy, but as a natural response to community involvement. As opposed to large corporations that often seek to enhance their reputations first and foremost, this motive is not the main priority for SMEs. Non-economic motivations for SMEs often go hand-in-hand with tangible benefits. SMEs usually show a commitment to supporting educational standards in their area, as any improvement in the local area will have indirect business benefits. SMEs can participate in fundraising initiatives, offer schools opportunity to visit their premises, and sustain engagement with community partners by sitting on the board of a school or charity and offering advice, or develop mentoring relationships with deprived pupils. Their relationship with local authorities improves and they strengthen links to other organisations. Owner-managers and their employees can form contacts that allow them to gain influence in the community and access to new business.

There are, however, limitations to how much SMEs can accomplish on their own. Problems related to economies of scale and constraints such as time, finances and human and technical resources may impede CSR efforts. They may also be at a disadvantage due to greater dependence on external forces in terms of technology or obtaining capital. Nevertheless, SMEs still have a certain flexibility that larger corporations do not have in that they are less bureaucratic and may deploy resources at their own will, making it easier to respond to community needs. SMEs often do not need to justify their actions to shareholders, nor do they need to develop a formal corporate strategy. They are often more innovative than larger corporations in their marketing or management approach and can adapt to situations and customise products to fit consumer needs and market demands. SMEs with strong community links may be better placed than large corporations in supporting community causes as they have greater commitment to the community, gaining directly from developments. Their detailed knowledge of the various organisations in the community and knowledge of the problems that need to be targeted often make SMEs willing to work with other firms in the community more readily than a large corporation as local ties make it easier to establish trust and sustainable relationships. SMEs can contribute to neighbourhood renewal because of their expertise in the locality and benefit through their desire to improve the local area for business gains.

SME owner-managers will still have to see some benefit to their business in order to engage and the benefits of being socially responsible need to be widely understood by SMEs. It is important that these owner-managers understand what criteria would make them engage in CSR and the need for coherence is essential for the SME sector. Some owner-managers believe that by helping society, they are helping themselves. Others may want proof of financial benefits. A support system needs to be in place to enable them to engage in a way that is both convenient and attractive. SMEs want to hear about the tangible benefits accrued by their peers and competitors. Information needs to be centralised and disseminated. Institutions that SMEs rely on for services (banks, for example) and the networks through which they conduct business and get support are ideal places for dissemination. Co-operation between these organisations should be encouraged. It should be clear that CSR can and does provide tangible benefits to the firm and those activities can be flexible according to their needs on the local level.

> *'To promote responsible business, the enthusiasm that exists in many small firms has to be recognised, harnessed and learnt from in order to create a framework to encourage more SMEs to follow suit.'*
>
> Ella Joseph

CSR and community development

The community is as much as a stakeholder as the other actors involved in CSR. People create communities and construct codes of conduct, reproduce meaning and values and build social trust in the form of social capital. Only when social trust and social exchange are well developed do communities engage in commerce and trade for the benefit of the community as a whole. In communities and countries that have a strong, well-developed third sector, capitalist markets thrive. Although some may insist that healthy economies create vibrant communities, the opposite is more often the case. A strong community is a prerequisite for a healthy economy, because it alone produces social trust. The transformation in the way commerce is conducted today is due to the transformation of relationships and the creation of communities.

Research and policy development focusing on the community and good corporate citizenship is becoming more and more prevalent. Internationally, Australian, British and American University based business centres have joined together to research corporate citizenship in order to draw attention to new projects and knowledge emerging within the field. Corporate citizenship is recognition that a business or business-like organisation has social, cultural, and environmental responsibilities to the community and that their goal should be to achieve long-term sustainable success for the community at large. The Boston College Center for Corporate Community Relations is the leading organisation helping corporations rethink their role in the community. Corporate involvement in community and economic development is growing with the funding for these initiatives often coming from business. Some of the current programmes include a project focusing on a strategic framework that helps companies to identify and approach corporate citizenship as a business strategy, appropriately called *Becoming a Neighbor of Choice* and an on-going project supported by the Ford Foundation on *Corporate Investment in Community and Economic Development.* The Ford Foundation ultimately would like to develop a model of strategic corporate involvement in underdeveloped communities. The Center is also working with the Hitachi Foundation on a programme that supports four non-profit intermediaries to work with business to develop mutually beneficial partnerships that uses employee volunteers. The principle mission is for all companies to act as social and economic assets to communities by integrating social interests with other business objectives.

When relationships are built that create trust in the community, the results create profits on several levels. An example of how this functions can be seen with Merck, one of the world's largest pharmaceutical companies. Merck uses a strategy called 'site-based community relations' in which managers attend community meetings and build relationships with influential members of the community. Upon moving headquarters, the company sent a community relations manager to the new site two years prior to the move. The manager interviewed neighbours of the proposed site and their requests led to design changes. The company was praised in a *New York Times* article for being receptive to community needs and the community continues to support the company's presence.

Box 6. The Body Shop: The Community Trade Programme

Socially responsible product sourcing can ensure that needs be met in the local communities.

The Body Shop International is a pioneer in the area of supporting long-term sustainable trading relationships with disadvantaged communities. In 1994, the corporation developed guidelines for Community Trade Partnerships and has since then, doubled their suppliers. Some of these suppliers are non-profit organisations, while others are for profit organisations that support their communities through charitable foundations.

An example of one of these suppliers is Teddy Exports in India. Through its charitable foundation, the Teddy Trust, they run a school, various AIDS awareness initiatives, as well as health and education services for employees and the local community. At times, the company not only buys products from a supplier, but also pays more in order to fund social programmes. Therefore, when the Body Shop buys hand-made paper products from General Paper Industries in Nepal, they pay an extra premium above the agreed price to fund the General Welfare Pratishtan, an independent trust to help the community in matters of health, education, and the environment.

Employee involvement

Volunteering has become a huge trend, where companies are backing their employees to volunteer. There are clear benefits to both the company and the staff, as team building is developed and the company's public image is enhanced. Employee volunteering is no longer a random act, but is becoming part of corporate strategy, carefully managed and controlled by companies. Cares Partnerships in the United Kingdom, (funded by Business in the Community) is based on an American scheme to promote volunteering opportunities in the community. In the United States, 25 cities participate and in New York alone, 10 000 participate (www.caresinc.org.uk). Cares Partnerships focuses on the idea of the community taking care of itself, with action on the local streets. This concept enforces a sense of ownership and each programme is run through a local partnership comprising business, the voluntary sector, local government, and other key community stakeholders. Visibility is achieved by adopting a high profile media approach that draws attention to volunteering and opportunities in individual communities, as well as recognising the corporate supporters. Business plays a major role in the funding of these programmes in both the United States and the United Kingdom.

Box 7. Polo Volunteers

The Polo Ralph Lauren Corporation offers Polo employees an opportunity to share their time and talents with local communities' organisations. Launched in February 2000, Polo Volunteers have dedicated hundreds of hours to local organisations. By partnering with small public schools, and organisations, meaningful connections are established between the employees and the community in which they work. The company strives to enhance their resources and effect change fostering a sense of belonging for all stakeholders in the community. Polo Volunteers teach art classes, cook hot meals, tutor students or spend time with the elderly.

The company also assists with Career Gear, a no-fee, non-profit organisation that helps to dress job seekers. Founded in 1999, Career Gear provides clean, interview appropriate clothing for men graduating from job-readiness programmes, affording them the 'outer confidence' needed for successful job interviews. This initiative helps men from all ages and backgrounds feel more positive about themselves and their futures.

The Cecile Network is a growing network of partnership organisations and companies dedicated to expanding employee community involvement in Europe. With partial funding from the EC, practical materials are being produced to help more employees get involved in tackling social issues. The network acts as a broker, providing a range of services to support the development of employee and community involvement through consultancy, workshops, providing business with insights into community needs and managing the relationships amongst different actors.

Collective action within the private sector can bring many benefits to these companies. The private sector does indeed have the capacity to work together non-competitively. This demonstrates responsible leadership, pools resources, and establishes programmes that can be long-term, helps to enhance the reputation of the private sector and participants in the business community. For other partners, a non-threatening environment is created for multi-lateral agencies, governments, and NGOs to engage with business. Partnerships with business gives access to a range of skills and experience not usually found in the public sector. The private sector can assist in ensuring that the investment of capital and time and energy is used to the best possible advantage, but one must avoid the risk of allowing public and private sectors from becoming too powerful and the community being excluded from decision-making on key projects. The consumers are also actors and need to be taken into consideration.

Trust is built through actions and allows for further co-operation in the future. A new environment is thus created for people to develop business and management skills and to use them in their communities.

Box 8. Levi-Strauss & Co: Giving back to communities

Levi Strauss & Co and Levi Strauss Foundation fosters positive change in communities where it has a business presence by awarding grants, encouraging volunteerism, and standing behind controversial issues. More than $16 million is donated annually in over 40 countries.

Levi Strauss contributions focus on four areas:

- **AIDS**: Providing funds to organisations working to prevent the spread of AIDS/HIV and care for those who are affected, including support services for the individuals and their families.

- **Economic Empowerment**: Supporting programmes that seek to improve economic opportunities for low-income people, particularly woman, minorities, the working poor, and other disadvantaged populations. The priorities of this area are: job creation, small business development, training and placement, and capacity building for non-profit organisations in order to assist them in economic development projects.

- **Youth Empowerment**: Supporting programmes that engage youth in decision-making, giving them a voice in the community, encouraging training in the media field, community service, and issued-based activism.

- **Social Justice**: Supporting those who are working to support basic human rights and combat institutional discrimination issues in mostly low-income areas. Funding is provided to non-profit organisations to do effective anti-racism work.

For Levi-Strauss, social responsibility and value-based business practices are the guiding strategy for the company. They stand behind some of the most controversial social issues because of their importance to the quality of community life.

Revitalising industrial areas

There are changes affecting class structure in industrialised countries. Today, less than 20 per cent of the workforce in most of the developed economies is in manufacturing, and this proportion is continually decreasing. The traditional working class communities, centred on coal, iron, and steel production have altered their character. Some areas have been revitalised while others have sunk into decline.

Responsible restructuring examples based on partnerships can be seen in France, the United Kingdom and Sweden following such changes in the workforce in these industrialised countries. In areas characterised by heavy industry, the challenge of redeployment of the workforce and overcoming environmental and social problems was accomplished through the creation of networks working in partnership with the local actors.

In France, SOFIREM (the Société Financière pour Favoriser l'Industrialisation des Régions Minières), was created in 1967 as a subsidiary of the Group of Charbonnages de France and became involved in industrial redeployment in traditional mining reasons affected by industrial decline. Major efforts were put into place in several zones, with particular intervention in the North of France, where SOFIREM acts as a service company as well as a financial partner. Their approach was an original one in France, taking responsibility in areas that would have not been able to survive if left alone, providing finance for inward investment and new business start-ups. In over 30 years, SOFIREM has invested 4 billion French Francs and has helped to develop over 100 000 jobs in coalfield closure areas, helping to finance and carry out 4 000 projects.

In the United Kingdom, a similar situation occurred in the steel industry. The British Steel Industry (BS(I)) Ltd. was established in 1975 as a subsidiary of British Steel to deal with the local economic problems brought about by the modernisation and the privatisation of the steel industry. In the period between 1975-1996, BS(I) created about 60 000 new jobs directly and about the same amount indirectly within the 20 areas that they helped to restructure in the United Kingdom. Like SOFIREM, BS(I) provides tailor-made packages to help fund SMEs and make use of financial instruments involving equity and providing loans at advantageous rates.

Jobs and Society (SJS) was founded in 1985 as Sweden's first enterprise agency in order to counter the effects of the shutdown of the Kockums steel plant. The initiative came about with the active participation of

Volvo, the local authorities and the business community. Jobs and Society helps regenerate Swedish trade and industry and promotes an entrepreneurial spirit. Since its creation, SJS has helped launch 21 000 SMEs, and the success rate it phenomenal, with more than 96 per cent surviving longer than 5 years, well above the EU rate of 50 per cent. Much of this is due to the expert help that is tailored to the needs of each start-up.

Additionally, in Italy, a similar problem emerged in 1995, where the Falck mills in Sesto San Giovanni closed down following the European Commission plan to downsize the steel industry resulting in the loss of work for over 1 500 people. Falck Group S.p.A. adopted a collective outplacement approach that was based on a series of actions set-up by a Corporate Board that was created to help employees involved in the restructuring process to find employment, either by moving to another company or by starting a new business. Falck signed a Social Plan, in co-operation with trade unions, focusing on training employees in order to update their skills, providing guidance and advice for new jobs either within the Group or elsewhere in the labour market, and encouraging entrepreneurship and enterprise creation. This initiative was a success, notably due to the involvement of the SMEs that were involved in the process. In total, 591 employees were relocated to other companies, 70 were able to be placed elsewhere in the Group, and 298 opted to set-up their own enterprise.

These examples all happened in a state industry, but the methods used here could be transferable to other sectors that might face major closures. In partnership with the local authorities, the private companies, financial organisations, and other local development agencies, these initiatives all foster strengthening local communities through local networks, helping to create new enterprises with financial support and advice to assist in the growth of SMEs. These groups share the goals of promoting ethical standards and battling against a culture of assistance by empowering individuals within the community.

Partnerships for social inclusion

A key trend in OECD countries has been the application of a partnership approach to design and deliver local development programmes. Strong corporate responsibility develops through effective communication and interaction between business, community and government and the third sector. All four of these sectors need to be addressed and social inclusion can only be achieved through partnerships.

Box 9. Global Citizen, Local Partner: Rio Tinto

The Rio Tinto Company was formed in 1873 to mine the ancient copper workings at Rio Tinto in Spain. Today, Rio Tinto interests in industrial minerals, coal, iron ore and aluminium span 5 continents, with headquarters in London. On a global scale Rio Tinto aims to be the best mining company in the world, but the company remains responsive to national and local issues, basing its policies on a tradition of social responsibility, contributing to the economic and social development of communities where it operates.

The company recognises that its presence in a region can accelerate social change and that it is fundamental to work in partnership with the community to best achieve the maximum long-term benefits. Taking into consideration the different systems of government, cultures and traditions, the company respects the local traditions and regulations and uses management to empower and facilitate communities to develop self-managed and sustainable projects. The group seeks to safeguard social and economic well being beyond the life of a mine.

The key principles followed in all of Rio Tinto's operation include mutual respect, active partnership, and long-term commitment. In order to best achieve community relationships, the company:

- studies the community and appraises attitudes, cultures and beliefs;
- implements activities to improve their relationship with a locality;
- submits and implements 5 year plans that include continued contact with government and community representatives, engaging in reviews of the Group's social performance.

Rio Tinto adheres to relevant international and national charters, codes of conduct and guidelines, as well as its own policies. The Global Mining Initiative is a programme that began in 1999 and includes the continuing participation of government, NGOs and industry associations in forums to discuss emerging debates, gain information and improve performance. This initiative ensures that the mining industry contribute to global transition and sustainable programmes for economic development.

The private sector is fast becoming a fully engaged partner in civil society and the community investment approach, focusing on business and business resources under long-term plans with attention on building capacity and inclusion, is the stage at which the battle against exclusion really takes place. Inclusion refers to a sense of citizenship to civil and political rights and obligations that all members of society should have, not just formally, but as a reality of their lives. It also refers to opportunities and to involvement in public space. Fighting poverty requires an injection of economic resources, but applied to support local initiative.

Fostering partnerships: examples of good practices

Ensuring social equality and an inclusive labour market requires the mobilisation of all sectors in society. The public-private partnerships have an important role to play in implementing strategies. Public-private partnerships are a central way the economy and society operate in many regions, and government plays a key role in ensuring the successful development of these partnerships. The Copenhagen Centre (TCC) in Denmark seeks to identify, develop and raise the profile of local partnerships with a strong public and business involvement as an answer to instances of social challenge at the local level. TCC runs a survey in a number of European countries to identify, develop and raise the profile of good partnership practices. The non-profit sector also can run policies on behalf of public authorities.

In Ireland, employers are making CSR part of their business practice under a joint government and employers initiative proposed in 1998, the Foundation for Investing in Communities. This joint venture was launched by the Minister for Social Affairs to assist in tackling social exclusion in Ireland. The key role of the Foundation is to provide a focus and increase recognition to businesses that make CSR a part of their business practice by promoting volunteering, making community involvement a management responsibility, and budgeting resources for these purposes. There is special emphasis placed on the needs of children in disadvantaged areas, and the Foundation encourages companies to adopt a Community Charter in which companies formally agree upon a policy of volunteering for their staff in support of communities as well as a pledged level of financial commitment.

In October 2000, Ministers of Ireland, the United Kingdom, Denmark and the Netherlands met to establish a network on the social responsibility of business. A joint statement was signed 'Government as Partners -- fostering public-private partnerships for an inclusive Europe'. This was significant as European governments are recognising the need to develop frameworks for effective public-private partnerships, as well as initiatives to scale-up and transfer experience on successful partnerships across Europe. This informal network will work to organise an ongoing discussion between governments and exchange experiences with the goal of further developing the dialogue with

European businesses. They also hope to extend the network at political and organisational level with the participation of other European governments.

The 'Observatoire sur la Responsabilité Sociétale des Entreprises' (ORSE or the Study Centre for Corporate Responsibility in English) was created in France and joins together private companies, financial managers, NGOs and professional organisations to work together in the battle against exclusion, exchanging best practice ideas amongst stakeholders. ORSE contends that corporations must respond to exclusion, providing service to the local social scene, and co-operating with local actors. The Centre's first elected chairman, Fréderic Tiberghien, is also Chief Executive of VediorBis, a temporary employment company in France. VediorBis makes use of its temporary agencies in the battle against exclusion, acknowledging that enterprise alone cannot respond to the phenomena of exclusion without the co-operation of the various local actors and other firms in order to surmount the difficulties in distressed areas. Seven out of ten candidates at VediorBis are long-term unemployed registered with the National Employment Agency. As these candidates are sometimes confronted with free periods of time in-between temporary work assignments, VediorBis offers professional training at these moments in order to ensure that the candidates maintain the skills required in their field, increasing their chances for employment. The company recently signed an agreement with the Social Fund for Local Development in Bordeaux allowing for long-term unemployed to create their own enterprises through low-rate micro-credits, as well as developing partnerships with public institutions and the National Employment Agency in France to assist in finding employment for handicapped people.

Strong partnerships between business and a service provider or government agency is a critical key to success, where both the public and private sector is committed to developing the workforce. In order to promote inclusion the private sector can employ locally and SMEs can contribute employment or training initiatives for excluded groups. Through employing locally, resources are re-routed back into the community for improvement; thus there are potential benefits for everyone. Companies can encourage workplace adaptability and flexible schedules as to secure employment for all individuals. In France, Danone offers a specialised home-care service for sick children so that mother's do not need to take time off. Electrolux Zanussi in Italy, has invested in IT equipment so that pregnant woman and new mothers can work from home, and offers flexible working hours where overtime can be converted into leave.

Providing opportunities

Supporting actions against exclusion extends over national borders. Auchan, a major supermarket chain in France with stores overseas has been supporting such actions since 1990. Based on the conviction that employment is the most effective tool against exclusion, an agreement was signed with their subsidiary Alcampo in Spain and the association for the blind (ONCE) ensuring that the Spanish store would hire 150 blind people by the year 2002. In France in 1996, the Fondation Auchan pour la Jeunesse (Auchan Foundation for Youth) was created with the assistance of the Fondation de France. The three areas of intervention include creating and supporting projects promoting employment, redeployment in rural areas, and health care for youth.

The Fundacion Empresa y Sociedad (FES) was founded in Spain in 1995 to encourage and promote corporate community involvement. FES is a business-driven organisation working with companies like IBM Spain, Citibank, and BP. FES emphasises the investment of technical and financial resources to aid social development projects, notably in the areas of welfare, health, education and vocational training. The Foundation provides consultancy services to corporations in order to help them to integrate CSR into their business strategy and helps long-term unemployed and individuals from ethnic minorities establish contacts and find work through the network of companies. Although the companies do not reserve jobs specifically for FES participants, they do allow them the chance for an interview, which in many cases would not have been possible without FES's intervention. Through the co-operation of the company and FES, potential candidates are offered training and advice to help identify and improve skills.

The example from the United States

In the United States, small business is a powerful engine of job growth, creating more than 75 per cent of the new jobs created in the mid-1990s. Businesses there have traditionally responded to community needs and have long been involved in CSR. Business began forming partnerships with non-profit organisations to strengthen communities through job training programmes and economic development. In 1996, the United States Congress passed the Personal Responsibility and Work Opportunity Reconciliation Act in order to change welfare policy in the United States. As a result of this Act, the Welfare-to-Work Partnership was created in 1997 as an independent, non-partisan organisation of the business community to help move people on public assistance to jobs in the private sector. Companies may benefit from subsidies through tax credits if they hire certain categories of welfare recipients, but they are also engaging in process that does have some risks and requires a comprehensive plan within the company in order for it to succeed.

An example of how small companies can engage can be witnessed in the case of EasyWeb, Inc. This small company, with two offices in North Carolina, specialises in Internet design and marketing. The company helps to prepare former welfare participants for jobs in the high-tech industry. Through partnerships with local government agencies, such as the Durham County Department of Social Sciences and private companies including GTE, EasyWeb created a training centre to attract candidates from the welfare population. EasyWeb itself has hired 7 employees from the training centre to join its staff of 18, and the company has placed over 130 former welfare recipients into jobs in the high-tech industry.

Community-based Welfare-to-Work efforts, those that bring together business, government and community-based organisation are the driving force behind local success. By working together, the public and private sectors can provide the resources, opportunities and co-ordination necessary to implement projects. In many communities, businesses have been the driving force behind moving people from welfare to work. In New Orleans, LA, a regional human resources director for McDonald's realised that most companies really did not understand how to put the Welfare-to-Work concept into practice. He organised other employers in the area, service providers and local government agencies to form an activist group to promote the programme to the business community. The group, known as the Employers Roundtable, included representatives from MNCs, regional companies, the local Private Industry Council and the State Department of Labor. The Roundtable created a forum of about 225 people in order to raise awareness and enlist business to hire welfare recipients. By partnering with the Department of Labor, the Roundtable has produced a how-to video for potential companies, and the Roundtable ensures that the private sector maintains a key role in having an impact on their community.

Some individuals are overlooked by employers, such as high-risk youth, the handicapped or former prisoners. Businesses that hire these workers can take advantage of Job Training Partnership Act Funds for training and can secure tax credits if the workers or the businesses are in a disadvantaged area. The hotel chain, Marriot International, adopted a programme, Pathways to Independence, moving people from welfare to their programme to jobs at Marriot. The programme trains these individuals and offers them full time jobs with benefits upon the completion of training. The company reports reduced absenteeism and tardiness and improved retention, as well as improved customer service with these employees.

Four years after the creation of the Welfare-to-Work Partnership, over a million people who were welfare recipients have been hired with full-time jobs. Government, business, and the non-profit sector working together was the driving force of this initiative and today it is a model of how problems can be solved through partnerships.

Expanding partnerships through information and telecommunications technologies

The convergence of information technology and telecommunications is creating a set of new sources of competitive advantage, but it is also widening the social divides and creating a knowledge 'underclass'. Internet provides both opportunities and challenges to business. It can serve as a central information source, but can maintain a local focus through multiple access points. The idea of using technology, (*i.e.*, the Internet) to spread awareness and knowledge of SME engagement of CSR can be seen with the Business Impact Taskforce of BT (British Telecom). The Taskforce acknowledges the need to involve smaller companies and have a website full of information where companies can learn from others' experiences. Government can also encourage SME involvement through good practice information. Linking local government sites with CSR information for SMEs can be efficient.

On both sides of the Atlantic, in both the United States and the United Kingdom, Microsoft has established taskforces in order to work with the small business sector to explore opportunities for better use of Information Communications Technology by SMEs (in the United Kingdom, they do this through Business Links). Most SMEs are involved in lower technological fields, such as manufacturing motor components or telecommunications equipment, which are susceptible to foreign competition. They make lack resources to improve their technical material, and without the assistance and expertise of a group like Microsoft, they would not be able to advance in the value-chain.

The European Commission's e-Europe initiative for the Summit in Lisbon was an important step for the EU in maximising the benefits of globalisation and technological advances. Objectives outlined in the e-Europe document include:

- 50 per cent of the European population should be able to have access to and use information and communications technology by the end of 2001;

- establishing a task force in which industry, training institutions, the Member States and the European Commission would consider how to meet the needs of the Information Society in Europe and collaborate with existing public and private initiatives;

- launching an appeal to European business to devise a joint Action Plan for Education as a key for economic competitiveness and social inclusion.

Access to telecommunications has transformed the lives of many communities and their economies through enhanced educational and enterprise opportunities created. The OECD countries make up less than 20 per cent of the world's population, but account for about 70% of all telephone lines. Despite the great strides surrounding telecommunications, over half of the world's population today has never placed a phone call. With governments around the world deregulating and selling their communications infrastructures, the private sector is becoming the arbiter of communication in the new economy. Voluntary initiatives and socially responsible practices of the telecommunications sector widen access to services within a framework of activity which engages with local communities on issues such as education, environment, health concerns and increased capacity to respond to emergencies.

An example of a telecommunications company working in partnership in a developing region can be witnessed in Bangladesh, where Telenor, a Norwegian telecommunication company became involved with the Grameen Bank by providing cellular headsets to rural micro-enterprises. This partnership helped Telenor win entry into Bangladesh and provide a distribution outlet for its product. Since Bangladesh have less than 3 phones per 1 000 inhabitants, it is an untapped market. This partnership not only offers new micro-enterprise opportunities for Grameen's members, but also helps improve the communications infrastructure that is critical to the development of both the company and the region.

'The idea goes way beyond social obligation. Its impact in communities is remarkable - families can make calls for the first time to migrant workers, it decreases transport needs, it creates jobs, and becomes an economic hub in very poor settlements.'

Kassiem Carrim, Head of Community Service,
Vodacom Group, Johannesburg, South Africa

Box 10. Connecting people as well as wire

Media One International, based in London, has developed a set of international properties in cable telephone and wireless communication. Their international arm is one of the largest broadband communication companies, providing access to the United States, Asia and Europe. As well as connecting wire, Media One is also connecting people.

The company runs the US West Foundation, which manages charity and grant-making programmes worldwide. The foundation invests millions of dollars annually in education, the arts, civic and community services, seeking to connect people by supporting programmes linked to schools through training teaches about new technological advances.

Connecting SMEs to information that they need to grow and create jobs and put all people and the organisations that serve them, in touch with resources than can improve their lives. Media One encourages and supports businesses owned by minorities and women

In Sweden, the Ericsson telecommunication group, is the country's biggest exporter. The company has recently formalised their social commitment through a programme called Ericsson Response. This programme was established in co-operation with the United Nations Development Program and OCHA (Office for the Co-ordination of Human Affairs) and the International Red Cross and Crescent Federation, in order to aid in reconstruction when communities are ravaged by natural disaster or catastrophes created by people themselves. With the support of local management, Ericsson employees in many parts of the world (Vietnam, Turkey, and Venezuela for example) have participated in social projects. In addition to the Ericsson Response initiative, Ericsson has made a commitment to supporting the use of technology in philanthropy through the Ericsson Internet Community Awards (ERICA) programme. ERICA is a philanthropic awards programme that promotes the community-building power of the Internet and provides valuable technological resources to non-profit organisations from around the world with undeveloped ideas for web-based solutions.

Government's role

Governments play in important role in encouraging firms to become more socially responsible. Firstly, regulation and legislation as well as fiscal policy can provide incentives for firms to partner either among themselves or with government to address social issues. The lessons from the experience of MNCs with corporate social responsibility can be useful to local economies Working together, MNCs and SMEs can more effectively put the business case for open, transparent markets, deregulation, liberalised trade.

Regulation and legislation clearly can create an enabling framework, facilitating the change in attitudes in a community and to help spread best practice. Through awards and fiscal schemes government can pass the message of CSR to the community as a whole. In contrast to the current situation in the United States, the debate on CSR focuses on reducing the tax incentives to corporate giving (rather than promoting tax incentives to good corporate citizenship) and reducing the bureaucracy and confusion bound-up in current taxation rules: simplify the giving process instead of fiscal incentives. Government should develop their role as mediator and foster relationships between different interest groups. By endorsing and promoting best practice, a coherent and integrated system may be developed and implemented (this can be done through media coverage, local press, and marketing).

In 1992, the United Kingdom's Department of Trade and Industry undertook an initiative to bring together all public support subsidies for small business into a national network of one-stop-shops. This initiative, Business Links, linked the local Chamber of Commerce, local development agencies, local authorities, and a team of Personal Business Advisors (PBA). The purpose of this network, which is currently functioning in several regions in the United Kingdom, was to have partnerships research their local markets and in order to develop long-term strategies. The key goals include:

- increase the role of SMEs in the community and to ameliorate customer relations in order to better meet their demands;

- raise the quality of service to SMEs;

- bring together the various organisations with emphasis on customer activities;

- maintain business support as an essential component in developing an economic development strategy for a locality.

This year, on 10 October, the UK government launched a £800 million Neighbourhood Renewal Fund, entering into a co-operation scheme with local companies as part of its strategy to improve local neighbourhoods and provides incentives to local councils to work with business.

Company involvement will be the main criteria for localities seeking funding and the government, as a way of encouraging local partnerships, provides support and advice to the local councils in order to achieve their goals.

Regional Development Agencies (RDAs) can help to promote CSR at the regional level to co-ordinate information, making sure that policy is coherent. Coherent and comprehensive policy for SME engagement in the region and encouraging partnerships with public, private and voluntary and community sectors will promote social inclusion. By acting as a broker at the regional level, larger companies located in the region can be approached and RDAs can encourage the CSR agenda, so that they become active in the community and form partnerships with SMEs. The London Enterprise Agency (LEntA) in London is making a great impact in the City in its role as broker in the community. LEntA's approach is firmly rooted in the private sector, enabling companies to work together on tackling social and economic problems. The agency has pioneered programmes that have served as test-pads due to their national, European, and international relevance in issues like ethnic diversity and homelessness. Concepts such as Invest a Saturday, where one-day training is provided for potential entrepreneurs, or the creation of LEntA Ventures, an informal venture capital arm that assists business to find equity through the support of Business Angels, have been fundamental to promoting job creation and inner city revival.

Conclusions

Collective corporate action provides a powerful mechanism, which enhances the ability of the business community, working closely with broader civil society, creating and supporting inclusion and a socially beneficial economic context. With closer stakeholder ties, business can collectively and individually with communities, labour, and NGOs define and implement innovative mechanisms for policy dialogue and work together on public-private partnerships at the local level. Because of the power behind the public and private sectors, the third sector and the community risk being alienated. Decisions should not be thrust on to a local community, and the members of the community need to get involved as active stakeholders and have a role in decision-making. By providing training and employment opportunities for excluded individuals, the opportunities for building sustainable livelihoods is greatly increased.

There is clearly a need for public and private entities to work together on solving societal problems. Partnerships between different segments of society require a detailed understanding of mutual expectations, resources available, organisational structures, and responsibilities. Working in partnership is a process that facilitates innovative solutions to meeting the social challenges at the local level. In order for partnerships to function, each partner needs to agree upon its mission. Trust is an essential element and different levels of power, whether political or financial, need to be addressed. The understanding of different methods (corporate vs. civil servant) is crucial to a co-operative and successful partnership and the different sectors need to be accountable to each other.

To encourage and stimulate new partnerships, public policy should be developed. This can be done through a balance of regulatory frameworks and market incentives. Regular meetings should be organised with government and business at the local and national level and concerned parties should invest in research into models of successful partnerships between companies, governments and communities. At the same time, using policies to promote inclusion is very complex. Policies need to be established into new systems of education, developed by both government and business working together. Government should engage in partnerships with private enterprise, giving corporations a role in activities, ensuring the public interest. Government needs to participate in making employment possibilities accessible by providing an infrastructure that corresponds to the needs of the individuals of the community - offering jobs in areas that cannot be easily reached because of inadequate transport facilities will not work. ‘Family-friendly’ workplaces should be encouraged and can be achieved through public-private collaborations (example: childcare, work sabbaticals). Governments that help companies with such issues will also tend to attract inward-investment in their locality.

PRESENTATIONS BY SPEAKERS

OF THE SECOND PART OF THE ROUNDTABLE DISCUSSIONS

STIMULATING PARTNERSHIPS WITH BUSINESS

AT THE LOCAL LEVEL

Partnerships and SMEs: Addressing Social Exclusion

Ella Joseph, Researcher, Commission on Public Private Partnerships, Institute for Public Policy Research (IPPR)

The role for the private sector in dealing with social exclusion

I would like to discuss how the UK Government sees the role of the private sector in addressing the linked problems of social exclusion and neighbourhood decline. Five related areas for business involvement have been set out for deprived areas:

1. delivery of government policy initiatives;
2. location and general business activity in deprived communities;
3. inclusion in public-private strategic partnerships;
4. provision of mainstream public services;
5. corporate social engagement activity that we are discussing today.

There are three related problems with this approach. Firstly, there is an exaggeration of the extent to which responsible business activity is already taking place and also the extent to which we can and should rely on the private sector in solving these problems. Secondly, there is confusion within the public and private sector about what the appropriate role of business is and what it has to offer. Thirdly, the motivation and potential benefits to engaging in the five areas outlined above vary and this creates problems for Government in developing a coherent message for business as to why it should be involved.

Thus, when looking at social exclusion and neighbourhood decline, there are four sectors or groups relevant to any discussion about policy that aims to address social exclusion and urban regeneration. There are the private sector, the public sector, the third sector, and the community and there is a complex set of links and relationships between them. Some of the obstacles to developing strong and mutually supportive links include culture, skills or the capacity to manage the relationship, the compatibility of organisations to work together, and rules (the barriers or obligations to effective engagement from legislation, etc.).

Policy themes

Social exclusion is a key theme for current UK policy. Year 1997 saw the establishment of the Social Exclusion Unit (SEU) at the heart of Government in the Cabinet Office. However, its meaning is widely contested and it is often argued to be too broad to be meaningful. My institute, IPPR understands it to include tangible problems such as poverty and low skills, as well as intangible problems such as alienation, stress and low aspirations. It can be geographically concentrated and can disproportionately affect certain societal groups, for example lone parents and the unemployed.

Neighbourhood decline is another key theme of the current Government (and overlaps with the theme of social exclusion). The Audit Commission summarises the concept of regeneration as '*a response to economic, social and environmental dereliction to promote prosperity and increase quality of life*'. There is a big overlap between these ideas and those encompassed by social exclusion. For example unemployment, skills and health can all be considered as measures of dereliction.

Recent UK policy focused on general corporate social responsibility. A CSR brief was given to the Department of Trade and Industry (DTI) minister for Consumer Affairs and Corporate Governance. It was widely regarded as a positive step that CSR was put with an industrial brief. However, until now the Minister's primary message to business concerns its reputation: the disastrous effects of being caught using child labour and the benefits of public relation boosts from community projects. This is a long way off promoting social engagement that is integrated into core business practice. He is extremely cautious about actually intervening in the market.

A Company law review (1998-2001) was also established. There is a proposal to extend the definition of company directors' responsibilities to include groups other than shareholders and a proposal to require companies to publish social and environmental regulation. The Review will not finish until next year, but it is widely thought that it will not reformulate directors' duties to reduce the primacy of shareholders, rather it will clarify that by giving other stakeholders due regard, directors will not be breaching their duties. This bias towards 'soft regulation' will do little to oblige companies to act more responsibly or to give consumers ammunition to force them to do so.

SMEs and corporate social engagement

IPPR research into the corporate social responsibility of small and medium sized enterprises (SMEs with less than 50 employees) found that there is a lot that can be learnt from smaller companies that is more widely applicable to larger corporations. How CSR manifests itself in SMEs helps to answer the question of what it means to be a socially responsible company and illustrates the type of engagement in addressing social issues that can be expected of companies. Research shows that those benefits previously thought to lie exclusively in the domain of large corporations are in fact replicated at the local level. Large corporations and government can and should support and facilitate the efforts of SMEs.

In its work on private sector social responsibility, IPPR has adopted the term 'corporate social engagement'. Corporate social engagement is defined as '*the methods by which businesses help promote social inclusion, through endeavours located both externally to their business, through engagement with other organisations, and internally by addressing exclusion directly*'. This highlights an inclusion approach, as what we are working towards today.

Whilst researching SME activities in this area we found that most of them adopted a holistic approach and did not consider this a community involvement strategy as such as large MNCs might. Their activities included sharing resources whether they are cash, products, surplus materials, facilities, or time, but also more integrated in their employment practice is the targeting of their opportunities. This includes employment (recruitment practices), experience (offering work experience), and access to goods and services (ensuring they do not exclude groups from consumption). The areas that SMEs are particularly interested in are education and regeneration and here they have the potential to make a real impact on local social problems.

It is widely acknowledged that evaluating the benefits of a social engagement strategy is an imprecise science. However, a number of benefits were highlighted by SMEs in the IPPR research:

- Creating a favourable business environment;

- Recruiting and retaining happy and quality employees;

- Public relations payoffs;

- Intangible benefits *e.g.*, personal satisfaction, especially where owners/managers had strong links to the community and conviction to contribute.

As Marie Donnelly said, SMEs make up an important sector in the EU and it is important that everyone recognises the benefits that we all associate with a large corporation are also replicated at a smaller level as well.

Corporate social engagement

Corporate Social Engagement (CSE) is an issue that cuts across numerous Government departments and government at all levels. The recommendations can only be effectively implemented via a co-ordinated response by:

- Central Government Departments;
- Regional Development Agencies (RDAs);
- The Small Business Service (SBS);
- Training and Enterprise Councils (TECs) and then Learning and Skills Councils (LSCs);
- Sectoral groups (including Trade Associations, Chambers of Commerce, Institute of Directors and CBI); and
- Local government.

I realise that this is very specific to the UK, but all of these bodies should see CSE as a legitimate business activity that is to be encouraged. They should work in partnership with the voluntary and community sector, learning from their experiences. Some of our recommendations include (and Marie Donnelly has made reference to some):

- Information has to be business-focused, flexible to individual companies' ability to help and flexible to their needs. Local and regional 'menus' of possible CSE opportunities should be easily accessible and clearly sign-posted to businesses;

- SMEs' CSE activities should be widely recognised and rewarded. Local areas and sectors should identify SME CSE-Champions.

There is a role for large corporations in supporting SMEs endeavours to be socially responsible and this could be done through the supply-chain. A few examples of such methods could be by encouraging local purchasing, using skills and capacity through mentoring small local firms in similar industry, creating links and offering advice and linkages with firms, and developing markets by using local firms as pilots for new technology. These are all possible strategies that could advance local economic development.

Stimulating public-private partnerships

Partnerships between the public sector and business or third sector organisations to deliver publicly funded outcomes (relationships encompassed by the term PPP) have an important role to play in mainstream service delivery and also in forming wider strategies. There are a number of possible ways to improve the engagement of the public, private and third sectors in partnership with each other and in order to encourage PPPs it is necessary for change to take place in all three sectors. This is achieved by ensuring that there is a level playing field in local service delivery for all sectors and partnership arrangements and by making sure that the public sector is a better partner, for example by separating accountability and leadership roles in strategic partnerships.

There is a wide range of ways in which the third sector can be supported as a potential provider of services, as well as a key player in setting local priorities and strategies. Firstly, there should be support the for third sector's capacity to bid for local service delivery contracts and play a role in nurturing these markets. Secondly, it is necessary to acknowledge the value of contributions in kind to strategic or regeneration partnerships and provide resources for all the key groups to play a role. There are numerous possible ways to enhance the motivation of the private sector to engage with the public sector at the local level, some more contentious than others are. The primary thing to do is to clarify the use of partnerships as the public sector is often unclear about what it hopes to achieve by engaging the private sector.

There are two possible reasons that linking the themes of PPPs and corporate social engagement it could be relevant to service delivery partnerships. First of all, it may influence whom the public sector chooses to deliver public services. If the service is publicly sensitive (*e.g.*, social care) then users must be able to trust providers and providers must be accountable. For example, accountability through social reporting and trust built up through reputation can be critical. Also, there is scope to require service providers to give some of their economic gains back to the community or at least support the community through employing locally and other such methods.

Empowerment to the Community through Partnerships

Marie-Françoise Wilkinson, Director,
European Anti-Poverty Network

The European Anti-Poverty Network is not just a Brussels based organisation, but we have 25 NGOs and 15 national networks, working against poverty and social exclusion in the Member states of the European Union, and to lobby for and with people and groups facing poverty and social exclusion. The work is mostly focused on EU experiences and includes monitoring and analysing Community policies, and lobbying the European Institutions for the adoption and implementation of policies and programmes against poverty and social exclusion. I agree with a lot of what the other speakers have said and particularly with Roy Jones of TUAC.

Responsibility to the workforce

I would like to put CSR in the framework of how companies run their business. There is a responsibility to the shareholders obviously, but there is a need for responsibility for other stakeholders and I see the workforce as the principle stakeholder. The responsibility of a company towards the workforce is to provide a safe working environment and workers' rights (including information and concentration rights), and providing fair pay. Like in the US, in Europe, we also find that a substantial percentage of the workforce is made up of working poor. Providing stable employment and constant upgrading of skills is extremely important so that the workforce can adapt to changes, as well as adopting anti-discrimination practises for women, older workers, minorities, the long-term unemployed. It has been noted that there is quite a bit of discrimination against those who have been out of the workforce of ran extended period of time, and trust deteriorates. There is also a need to hire people at their appropriate level of qualification, as we have noted that lower qualified employees may be penalised by the recruitment of new over-qualified staff.

Responsibility towards the community

Responsibility to contractors and suppliers is important in the North-South context. Firms need to provide quality products and services as well as free information. Regarding the wider community there is environmental responsibility and the need for sustainable development and social responsibility towards the community. In this respect companies should provide more training and apprenticeship opportunities for people in the community, employing people from local communities as often as possible and perhaps a clause should be introduced, a sort of public contract to ensure this. They should provide work experience and mentoring for those who have been excluded for a long time from the labour market and a partnership approach should be developed with the wider community.

Partnerships could be formed for with community enterprises in which technical assistance, the know-how of their workforce, and some financial assistance could be provided. I would like to stress that although these ideas are often very welcome by NGOs, any form of financial assistance should not substitute inputs from the already existent public and social services that should remain, first and foremost, the responsibility of the public authorities. I do not believe that firms should step in where public authorities fail. Social services are the responsibility of the public authorities as well as upholding the fundamental rights of peoples, and philanthropy cannot do this. The non-profit private sector can run policies on behalf public authorities. At least in European countries, they can provide welcome support for novelty projects set up by NGOs that do not always initially receive favourable treatment from public authorities. Therefore, it is important that this source of funds be used by the voluntary sector and community organisations.

Fostering partnerships

It is, once again, through a partnership approach that decisions may be made with local communities with the aim of responding to local needs. In this respect it is possible to maintain a long-term relationship, and not just a relationship based on a certain action. Time needs to be allotted for discussion and debate over the different viewpoints between those who are funded and those who are funding. Members of the community should feel free in expressing their opinions and concerns and both parties must understand that solutions can be found that are beneficial to all actors involved. In conclusion, social responsibility lies first and foremost in the way in which business is run. Philanthropy cannot buy a clean bill of health for companies that do not respect all stakeholders and in order to succeed in community involvement, companies should adopt a partnership approach, thus empowering the people and tackling social exclusion.

Applying the Broker Model in London

Andrew Carter, City Action Manager
LEtnA Trust

I would like to discuss how corporations get involved in CSR and what issues they are concerned about. The field of corporate social responsibility is huge and the huge agenda is actually part of the problem It is an overwhelming subject matter and the size of the agenda and the differing views are preventing us from tackling the issues at hand in order to effectively advance. We need to think about these issues geographically across the globe, sectorally across industries and thematically concerning the different areas we get involved in.

The LEtnA approach

LEtnA (The London Enterprise Agency) is based in London and is a subsidiary of Greater London Enterprise (GLE). We are a private sector partnership of 13 multi-nationals that work primarily in economic development and employment issues. From our experience, we see three particular models of how a company can get involved. Firstly is through direct corporate involvement where companies have a local presence. This occurs either through the fact that they have headquarters based there, they draw labour from the local market, or they purchase locally. The second model is through community partnerships based on a business core. In this case, a corporation usually sees an opportunity for new markets or new clients and thus they try to get involved in the community by working with community partnership projects, thus customising their products to the community's needs. The third and final option is engagement with the community through intermediary organisations or brokers. Brokers here act as a bridge between the community world and the corporate world. They have the expertise at hand in order to bridge the obvious differences that exist between theses two worlds.

Main areas of activity

LEtnA has four primary core areas of activity encompassing education, employment, entrepreneurship and enterprise development, and regeneration.

- Education includes the preparation of young people for work, getting private sector companies to work with excluded individuals and excluded people in schools to get them more involved and to work with individuals to help them to develop their life skills.

- Employment focuses on connecting people to jobs, focusing activities on excluded housing estates in London, and how to better introduce them into the mainstream market and mainstream labour market in particular.

- Entrepreneurship and enterprise development are key goals and this functions as sort of an investment matchmaking service in order to overcome exclusion. Often the funds and expertise are just not available to those who may have some very good ideas. Without the necessary resources, some of these ideas may never come forth.

- Regeneration, the final activity, entails looking at the role of corporations and the private sector in overcoming market failures in some areas and how their core activities relate to that.

Brokers at work -- City Action

An example of a broker at work is City Action, which is run by LEtnA. It is a joint venture between LEtnA as the broker and the corporation of London, which is London's local authority. The idea behind this venture is to promote or increase business involvement in specific community projects. We developed a series of options that we present to corporations that are considering getting involved in their local community or local community projects and to work through with them on how they can best proceed. A structured programme of engagement for companies may include a variation of the following:

- Board members: this might include presenting management opportunities to local people or having private sector representatives sit on school boards, or boards of community projects to offer their expertise and knowledge.

- Mentoring: LEntA provides advice and personal support in schools and private companies; working with individuals and providing them with often personal development assistance, at times even more so than professional.

- Volunteering: corporations get involved in their localities, whether it be forging new initiatives or redoing a playground, or painting premises. There is also the offering of expertise, which basically is the idea of using expertise of a particular corporation to go forward with a community project. This usually occurs in legal or financial fields.

- Providing goods and services: providing premises and office space that community projects can use to organise or host members in developing ideas in a new and different environment is important. There is a wide range of needs to fill, as in office equipment, updated IT, desks, photocopiers, wastepaper bins, etc.

- In house corporate training: courses on basic management skills, computers, and bookkeeping for local community leaders have been extremely successful.

Advantages of the broker model

The broker model is a way in which corporate social responsibility is conveyed on the local level. City Action acts as a broker between what the corporations can offer and what the communities want and need. It has been a success in London and it is an expanding activity.

Corporations and community leaders find the broker model to be an attractive choice for several reasons:

- By pulling resources together for a greater impact, the role of the corporation is enhanced in the community and community leaders have the opportunity to gain expertise.

- The broker can be used as a soundboard for new ideas without having to hire new staff for this.

- Links are further provided to communities.

- Risk management and decreased political visibility.

- In the past, corporations did not get involved in many community projects as they were concerned about the risk of failure, but using the broker is a safe way to test new ideas.

- Identifying new business opportunities.

Using a broker as a R&D agent to test new ideas and develop new products that can then be taken back to the corporations and developed across the corporate organisation. Corporations can get involved in a range of projects that perhaps they would not if they were standing alone or would not be able to do so, especially in projects that do not reflect their exact business needs. Through the broker, the corporation can get engage with indirect aspects in the community.

- It is a conduit for them to become involved in government policy, to influence government policy as well as to deliver and change government policy.

The support of the broker is necessary in order to achieve that. This again has been a successful model in fostering corporate social responsibility in the community.

Overcoming the Closure of the Coal Mines through Active Partnerships for Local Development

Jean-François Rocchi, Chief Executive Officer, SOFIREM

Coping with the closing of the coal mines

For the past 30 years in France, the coal mining regions have been coping with economic problems related to industrial redeployment and economic restructuring. The discontinuation of mining, competition from other forms of energy, as well as the increased cost of production, and the exhaustion of certain mining deposits have led the French government, since 1963, to progressively reduce the production of coal.

The company that I represent, SOFIREM (Société Financière pour favoriser l'industrialisation -- Company for the Industrial Redeployment and Economic Restructuring of the Mining Regions) is a subsidiary of the industrial group Charbonnages de France. In 1967, Charbonnages de France, in direct collaboration with the state, established our organisation with the purpose of acting as an economic development agency in order to facilitate the redeployment process. We became socially responsible in these areas because there was not a choice. Our mission consists of facilitating the implantation and development of French and foreign companies in traditional mining regions affected by industrial decline. We are a rare example in France in regards to our intervention, and the company will be dissolved in 2005. There was and continues to be a moral obligation to fulfil, as well as geographical and environmental problems to overcome, and we were allotted a certain period of time to accomplish our tasks. The closing of the mines encompasses human, economic, and cultural consequences that are all interdependent. We were faced with the necessity to recreate a principally industrial activity in these regions in order to ensure the continuation of a presence that the community was already accustomed to.

The role of SOFIREM in a local network

SOFIREM acts as a service company as well as a financial partner. As a provider of services, SOFIREM studies all the aspects of investment in a project in order to evaluate its needs, to help in choosing the most favourable site, to elaborate or complete a development plan, and to start-up the project by easing the administrative steps, and obtaining financial assistance. As a financial partner, SOFIREM directly participates in the financing of projects, providing loans at advantageous rates or by contributing funds in the form of minority and temporary shares under a joint account. The results of these actions are important even if there still is a lot to accomplish. In total there are more than 4,000 firms that have been listed resulting in a global sum of over FF4 billion of financing, thus more than 600 million. Over 12 000 new jobs have resulted from these projects. It goes without saying that these projects are carried out in close collaboration with the territories where they are taking place.

The local authorities, the regions, the towns, the Chamber of Commerce, the local development agencies, private companies and financial organisations are all national partners and nothing could be accomplished without this network.

We need to take the individual organisations of each zone into consideration in order to adopt a plan to the local context. There are a dozen zones of intervention and each one of then has their own organisation, their own culture and history that must be taken into account, while sharing the common factor that they were all marked by the presence of the coal mines.

In the territories where there is already system in place we dispatch a representative who works with the local network there. If we find that the network in place is not sufficiently fulfilling its role in serving the locality, we install an associative structure created in partnership with the local communities, the Chamber of Commerce and local firms to further incite the development and launching of an effective network. This procedure was applied in the South of France in Albi and Alès. Inversely, in the North of France, in the region of Nord-Pas-de-Calais, our subsidiary FINORPA works in liaison with the local representative of the French agency for territorial planning (the DATAR) and different structures put in place by various local communities. The Lorraine is a particular example, as area the of Houillères still had maintained a certain amount of strength in the area and it played a significant role in the economic impetuous that allowed us to act directly in creating a network that was beneficial to the region.

The inclusion through partnerships

I would like to say a word about the implication of the enterprise in the policies of 'positive discrimination' in favour of the local labour force. As I already mentioned, Charbonnages de France will stop its production in 2005 and will no longer be hiring personnel. It is through other means, like employment of youth and women that we can attempt to re-organise the labour market for people from these territories undergoing redeployment. This is really a battle against a culture of assistance towards the promotion a culture of co-development. The Fonds d'Industrialisation des Bassins Miniers created in 1984 and managed by Charbonnages de France, supports new programmes in the labour market, notably through professional training. It is difficult to take this much further as French law forbids the possibility of reserving jobs for certain categories of individuals, with the exception of the handicapped.

Our task is thus quite delicate, as we need to achieve this redeployment process in the next few years, with diminishing forces. The key to our success is finding links through the existing networks so that they may ultimately be transferred to the territories. The forms in which the transfer takes place will invariably differ amongst localities. Thus, I repeat that the partnerships established are essential to the creation of transferable instruments and the sustainability of our actions. One of our reasons for joining the LEED Partners' Club was to spread our ideas and methods in order to promote the continuity of our work. Each territory is a unique entity and it establishes it own network. This should be a growing process of the territory in co-operation with the network, and not the artificial importation of a ready-made model.

Welfare-to-Work: a Smart Solution for Business

Rodney Carroll, Chief Operating Officer,
Welfare-to-Work Partnership

Welfare Reform in the United States

Thank you for inviting me to join you at this esteemed gathering to share some thoughts about welfare reform in the United States. As many of you know, we are currently engaged in a great experiment to integrate many of our long-term unemployed citizens into the workforce. For decades in America, we have had what can only be described as a socio-economic 'underclass' -- an identifiable group of people who have been left out of the American mainstream.

Now, I am not a long-time welfare reform expert. For all of my life I had seen how our dysfunctional welfare system trapped millions of Americans in a vicious cycle of poverty and dependence. What I knew most about the welfare system in America was what *most* people knew about it -- that it didn't work. And if the reality isn't bad enough, the public's perception compounded the situation. The actual money spent on our welfare system -- $16.5 billion this year -- was a mere pittance of our $10 trillion Gross Domestic Product. That's barely two tenths of a percent. So at its heart, the problem was less about money than about values. People in America linked welfare with failure. Those on the rolls were stigmatised. They didn't play by the rules.

The need to changing the system

A temporary helping hand became for too many a way of life. This is a long way from the roots of the welfare system envisioned by President Franklin Delano Roosevelt 60 years ago -- a short-term safety net for families who'd fallen on hard times. We in America were more than embarrassed. We were horrified by a system in which parents lost hope in the present and children lost a chance at a future. This dynamic is what prompted President Bill Clinton to call for an 'end to welfare as we know it,' and what made possible a historic agreement between a Republican Congress and a Democratic Administration.

So in the summer of 1996, Congress passed, and the President signed, the Personal Responsibility and Work Opportunity Reconciliation Act. It was a sea change for welfare policy in our country.

The number of people affected by the change in America was huge. The new law targeted more than 4 million households and more than 12 million people. The total, in short, was almost 5 per cent of our population -- and excludes millions of non-custodial fathers, which makes the real percentage substantially higher.

The law ends cash assistance as a matter of right. It puts time limits and a work requirement on almost all welfare recipients. It gives welfare money to the states in regulated block grants, not an open-ended, never-ending spigot of money. Welfare recipients can receive benefits for up to five years during their lifetime -- and for only two consecutive years, or even less at the state's option. And while they are receiving benefits, recipients must be either looking for work or training for it. They must be actively seeking gainful employment. The work requirements are strict, but at the same time, eligibility for food stamps and Medicaid, our health care system for the poor, remains -- so there is still a basic, if modest, safety net in place. The key to the whole system is getting people into the workforce and into the economic mainstream.

The Welfare-to-Work Partnership

When he signed the legislation, however, President Clinton recognised that a change in government policy would not be enough to unwind 60 years of social problems. He recognised that a series of severe sanctions had to be joined with opportunities. As he put it at the bill signing: '*Every ...person in America tonight...who has ever said a disparaging word about the welfare system should now say, 'Okay, that's gone. What is my responsibility to make it better?*'

And that is where The Welfare-to-Work Partnership comes in. Conceived in early 1997 and launched with the full blessing of the President in May of that year, The Partnership is a completely independent, non-partisan organisation of the business community. That's right: Government is not involved in The Partnership. We have the endorsement of key public officials of both parties. In fact, our Advisory Board is chaired by Republican Governor

Tommy Thompson of Wisconsin and Governor Tom Carper, a democrat from Delaware, but that's it. '*Good luck*,' they said. '*Now it's up to you.*'

This independence might have weaknesses, but if so, I haven't seen them. It has allowed us to adopt a simple mission: to help companies hire and retain former welfare recipients and other Americans facing sever hardships. It has allowed us to adopt a simple method: we would motivate businesses to hire people off welfare and once motivated, we would educate them using best practices, financial incentives, and available resources. And it has allowed us to adopt a series of comparatively simple quantitative measurements of success: How many people have our companies hired? What are their wages and other benefits? For how long have they been retained against industry standards? Are they being promoted?

We started The Partnership with four assumptions:

1. *The first was the one your organisation has asked me to address today: That real public-private partnerships are critical to a truly successful Welfare-to-Work programme. Business, service providers and government all working together to move people from lives of dependence to lives of independence.*

   We could motivate and educate and tally successes and failures, but without government's wage subsidies, training money and tax incentives, and without its commitment to change local welfare offices from income maintenance centres to job creation centres, we could not succeed. So, instead of arrogance, we committed to dialogue and partnerships.

   In the United States, community-based organisations or service providers -- your version of *intermediaries* -- are the critical link between businesses who are looking for workers and welfare recipients who are looking for a job. Service providers come in all shapes and sizes -- job training sites, temporary staffing firms, faith-based organisations, job-readiness firms, community colleges, Goodwill, the Salvation Army, the YMCA -- from national organisations with proud traditions to feisty grass roots start-ups. From non-profits to a smattering of for profits to governmental welfare offices themselves.

   For too long, service providers had not been getting the job done. They have been the willing beneficiaries of government and private largesse, but somehow their training and readiness programmes have not been connecting with the human resource needs of the business community.

For example, Amy Betanzos, the founder of Wildcat Service Corporation, a for-profit intermediary based in New York City, points out that just a few years ago, she would sometimes train potential computer operators for 21 months and in the end, she still could not get them into the workforce. Finally, she realised that she had two customers: the welfare recipient and the business. She went directly to a prominent stockbroker house called Salomon Smith Barney and said, '*I will deliver you people, if you tell me what skills they should have.*' Salomon Smith Barney helped her train people for jobs in the financial service industry: Training in the use of equipment, in skills, office culture and vocabulary. Suddenly welfare recipients found good paying jobs while Salomon Smith Barney found dedicated, enthusiastic employees. It was that simple. So every 16 weeks for two years, more former recipients joined the ranks of the company with full benefits, stock ownership and an average entering salary of $24 000. And two years after the programme began, Salomon Smith Barney confirms a substantially lower turnover rate among its Wildcats graduates than from amongst its other entry-level employees.

The change in the welfare law in 1996, coupled with an unprecedented across the board labour shortage, created a historic opportunity for American business. But not before business, government and non-profit job training organisations learned to work together.

2. *The second assumption was that if a company committed to hire and retain former welfare recipients, then they would in fact hire and retain. To that end, we recruited five of America's most successful businesses to join The Welfare-to-Work Partnership by committing to hire and retain at least one person from welfare.*

Those five companies -- United Airlines, United Parcel Service, Sprint, Burger King and Monsanto -- were joined by 100 other businesses to launch The Partnership. At the launch, each and every business pledged before the President and their fellow Americans to hire and retain at least one former welfare recipient.

No business was asked to lower its standards. There was to be no displacement of existing workers -- we did not want the labour unions to feel threatened. We were only asking that businesses give Welfare-to-Work a chance.

3. *The third assumption was that the business community would be more inclined to go forward if we were to position Welfare-to-Work as a smart solution for business, rather than if we put it in terms of corporate responsibility or philanthropy. But I can tell you for sure, if Welfare-to-Work was not helping businesses grow, they would not be doing it.*

Welfare-to-Work is not about charity. It is about improving the bottom line. In a growing economy, many industries are facing a shortage of entry-level workers. And given current projections, that trend shows no sign of abating anytime soon in my country. And while we had no idea when we made the assumption, former welfare recipients are proving to be more than just a good source of entry-level employees. The statistics show that they are staying on the job. And that translates into bottom-line benefits for businesses.

Large companies as diverse as Marriott International, Bank of America, Xerox and T.J. Maxx have found that their retention rates for Welfare-to-Work employees are actually higher than retention rates for more traditional entry-level employees. That means Welfare-to-Work can lead to a more stable workforce. And this is more than just the large well-known companies of our country. According to a recent survey of our Business Partners, 65 per cent report that former welfare recipients are staying on the job as long or longer than other entry level employees -- up from 48 per cent in Spring 1998.

4. *Our final assumption was perhaps the most challenging. We reasoned that we would need to change attitudes before we could change behaviour.*

Changing business perceptions

Welfare was a system that was viewed as rotten. Welfare recipients were viewed as opportunists who had more children to avoid an honest day's work, while the truth was that the average welfare mother had just two children. Welfare recipients were viewed as overwhelmingly black, while the truth was that there were as many people on the rolls who were white. Welfare mothers were thought of as very young, while the truth was that only 7 per cent were teenagers.

So to change attitudes and perceptions we created a Public Service Announcement campaign -- in print and on the radio and television. We publicised statistics that debunked the common stereotype of the welfare queen. For example, the truth is that:

- 58 per cent of adult welfare recipients have completed the equivalent of high school or a higher level of education.

- Two of every three women on welfare have had some recent work experience.

- And, only a small minority of families on welfare have been on the rolls indefinitely; many, in fact, have received aid for less than two years.

As more and more businesses hired and retained former welfare recipients, the word started to spread. Businesses found workers and welfare recipients found jobs. Today, those five businesses have grown to more than 22 000 Business Partners all dedicated to hiring and retaining former welfare recipients. Companies from Wall Street to Main Street: all regions, all sectors, and all sizes. In fact, two thirds of our Partners employ less than 250 people.

We started The Partnership as a cheerleader, but we have quickly evolved into an educator and a facilitator -- one that brings all the critical components to one place at one time and creates motivated task forces that do the hard work of Welfare-to-Work from the ground up. We have followed this simple script and almost four years later we are proud of the fact that we are succeeding. According to a prominent American survey firm, our Business Partners are doing more than just signing their name to a piece of paper -- they are hiring welfare recipients -- more than 1.1 million former welfare recipients in the last three years. That is right, our Business Partners hired more than 1.1 million people from welfare -- primarily full-time jobs with health benefits and high retention rates. And even we were surprised when we learned that over 80 per cent of our Business Partners said that former welfare recipients were 'good, productive employees,' and that over 30 per cent could already report at least one promotion.

Overcoming barriers…slowly

I am happy to tell you that Welfare-to-Work is working in the United States. Not perfectly, to be sure, not equally across the United States and not without many hiccups. But the data speaks for itself: the welfare rolls are down sharply all across the country -- many states have actually cut their rolls in half, and most of the adults who have 'graduated' from the welfare rolls are working at least part time. Those who work for the member companies of The Partnership earn an hourly $7.80 -- not a king's ransom, to be sure, but well above our national minimum wage of $5.15.

We are not simply ending welfare as we know it. We are helping people reclaim their independence and make a better life for themselves and their families. But the job is not yet done. There is no question but that the challenges ahead are enormous. Too many of those left behind have severe barriers to overcome. There are language and literacy hurdles for many, problems of addiction, mental health and abusive relationships for others. And once they take those first tentative steps, success is not guaranteed -- not with over 30 per cent of those leaving the rolls still falling back on welfare before long.

Going into this, we all knew it would be tough -- 60 years of a failed social programme would not be ripped asunder in 60 days, or 60 weeks, or even 60 months. But the passing of legislation, a strong economy, continued innovations at the state level and the work at The Partnership convince me that we are locking in the gains of recent years.

Today, millions of Americans are getting invaluable experience, those whose families have been on welfare for generations, are getting a taste of what it's like to earn a paycheck. The problems will not be solved overnight, and they will not be solved by government or business alone, but through partnerships.

Let me call your attention to the words of our greatest President Abraham Lincoln, whose simple eloquence captures the essence of our mission. '*No great nation,*' Lincoln said, '*can sustain in idleness more than a small percentage of its numbers. The vast majority must labour at something productive.*'

What we are doing collectively is bigger than just one job at one company, although that is the building block, the foundation for all our efforts. We are engaged in work that will change our country for generations to come.

Combating Exclusion through Partnerships

Frédéric Tiberghien, Chief Executive Officer, VediorBis and Chairman of the Observatoire sur la Responsabilité Sociétale des Entreprises

Stakeholders against exclusion

Multiple demands are being placed upon the corporate world today, and an enterprise can no longer act or react without taking their stakeholders into consideration. I am referring to employees, suppliers, clients, shareholders, and people living near the production lines. The questions concerning social exclusion in the enterprise needs to be addressed, notably concerning their recruitment policies. We question whether it is the role of the enterprise to reduce inequality and fight against exclusion, or is this role first and foremost that of the state and the collective territories? A number of enterprises adopt an intermediary solution; while they do not pretend to replace the state in this function, they support the accessibility of jobs and training for excluded people.

ORSE

In the United States, certain investment funds specifically choose to invest in the companies that work in partnership with their stakeholders and the community. Over the last few years a number of networks have been attempting to develop the notion of a socially responsible corporation and socially responsible investment. Last May, VediorBis, along with 20 listed corporations, was at the origin of the creation of ORSE, the first network in France covering CSR. The Study Centre on Corporate Responsibility (ORSE, Observatoire sur la Responsabilité Sociétale des Entreprises) reunites companies, as well as investors, pension funds, unions and other professional associations with the primary objective of raising awareness of the corporations concerning their responsibility and to favour what we are calling ethical funds. These funds are predominantly invested in corporations that are environmentally and socially responsible, and this sort of investment is increasingly seen as a means of addressing the effects of globalisation. Today, these funds represent about 13 per cent of sums invested in the United States and have been in constant progression for the last ten years. We at ORSE think that this method will quickly catch on in Europe and we want to be prepared.

The Study Centre serves as a place of exchange amongst different stakeholders. If the people involved in ORSE come from different cultural backgrounds, this does not prevent them from working together towards a common goal, and we associate certain NGOs in our work. For example, we had the participation of a representative from Amnesty International at a recent meeting, which allowed for enterprise representatives to become aware of the interest and concerns of NGOs toward corporations. At the same time, the representative of Amnesty International was able to evaluate the degree of involvement of the corporations in regards to social issues.

A few years ago, the collaboration between such diverse groups would not have been possible. It was often considered as trivial by the enterprise, or something that only concerned the communication policy. The associations, on their side, systematically refused all contact with the corporations. Today partnerships have developed in all fields, in particular when the associations participate on the board of directors of cabinets of social rating or when an NGO participates at the launching of a product deemed socially or environmentally correct.

Corporations engaging locally

Amongst the obstacles to overcome in order to put into place a sort of collaboration between the NGOs and the corporations in the battle against the phenomena of exclusion in large cities, we must first identify the obstacles and then try to find the solutions. Cities are not generally counted amongst the stakeholders, and the corporations who had, up until the end of the industrial era, contributed to build the city and to invest, have in some ways, deserted this to the era of industrial restructuring, the displacement of their manufacturing and to enter in the service economy or/and training.

Without redoing Clermont-Ferrand, the Creusot, or Montbeliard in France, the corporations become part of the city. This is not very obvious in the 21st century. The corporations, public or private must respond to phenomenon of exclusion whole bringing necessary services to the social scene locally: public services (schools, day-care centres and health centres) but also local services para-public services in their proximity (post office, banks, local shop-owners, employment agencies or temporary employment agencies). This implies that there is co-operation with the local actors, publics and semi-public, as an isolated corporation cannot overcome alone the all of the difficulties encountered, particularly in distressed areas.

Beyond this, the corporations often respond to problems of exclusion through a form of charity. Certain distributors that install in supermarkets (Auchan or Carrefour for example) in distressed neighbourhoods also support local associations, intertwining their commercial presence through the social fabric as well. Several corporations encourage their own employees to participate in charitable acts or to invest in humanitarian causes (an example of this is AXA Insurance, which is encourages employees to participate in local or humanitarian causes).

The role of VediorBis

VediorBis is a temporary employment agency implanted locally and had put a training and insertion programme into place for their temporary employees. As the labour market fluctuates and employment contracts diversify, employers are more aware of the importance of life long training for employees. During the time periods when employees are not working on a temporary mission assignment, the temporary employees of VediorBis receive training in order to maintain professional skills sought out by the corporations, constantly reinforcing their employability. Temporary employment agencies have contributed to the battle against exclusion and have helped these individuals to get a new start. At the same time, VediorBis has established agreements with the Agefiph concerning handicapped employees and with the National Employment Agency (ANPE) in order to assist with the placement of unemployed people (7 out of 10 people who go to VediorBis are unemployed coming from the ANPE).

Our main goal is the battle against exclusion and recently in Bordeaux, we signed an agreement with the Caisse Social de Developpement Local, the Social Fund for Local Development. This is a rare initiative in France promoting entrepreneurship that allows for the excluded to fund their own enterprise thanks to micro-credits at very low rates.

PART 3

LINKING ETHICS AND FINANCE TO FOSTER SOCIAL RESPONSIBILITY

Overview of discussions

The third part of the roundtable focused on financial investments as a driver of CSR. Financial institutions such as savings banks as well as non-traditional financial institutions play an important role in communities, not only as a source of finance to companies and consumers but also as drivers of corporate social responsibility. Like other firms, financial institutions cannot just be responsible to themselves, their role goes beyond what they do as corporate entities insofar as they act as operators and guardians of socially responsible investment. In this vein, socially responsible investing (SRI), or ethical investing has grown in importance at the behest of both companies and consumers. The use of metrics such as social or environmental ratings in making investment decisions has gained momentum in the last few years as people increasingly put their money behind their values.

Indeed, at the Lisbon Summit of March 2000, heads of state explicitly lauded the role of the financial sector in providing the means for both economic and social development and recommend that the financial sector recognise its responsibilities to the community at large and promote socially responsible investing.

... 'The financial sector has a key role in providing the means for both economic and social development. It is, therefore, vital that current and future finance leaders be fully aware of their responsibility to allocate capital so as to support job creation, entrepreneurship and local regeneration. In recognition of the special role of capital resources in achieving employment and social goals, we recommend encouragement of the financial sector to widen access to its services, recognise its responsibilities to the entire community and promote socially responsible investing.'...

One clause of the Appeal made at
the Lisbon Summit of the Council of Europe,
March 2000, specificially directed at the financial sector.

Socially responsible investing

The notion of socially responsible investing (SRI) emerged in the 1960's. Then the focus was on promoting socially responsible investment in international investments, in particular in protest of investments in South Africa during the period of apartheid. Environmental considerations also began to be considered in investment decisions. Over the past five years, there has been tremendous growth in the field of SRI, very much linked to the upswing in CSR. Public consciousness of ethical issues and their linkage to investments is affecting the way companies conduct business. In the United States, Social Investment Forum data from 1999 showed that nearly one out of every seven dollars under investment management in the United States -- more than $2 trillion -- is now actively involved in the corporate social responsibility movement. Remarkably, socially responsible assets grew at twice the rate of all assets under management in the US, linked in part to increased participation of defined-benefit and defined-contribution. In the UK, the first ethical trust was launched in 1984, Friends Provident Stewardship, which originated from Friends Provident, a large mutually owned life insurance company set-up in the 1830s by Quakers. Since 1984, over 40 new ethical unit funds have been created in the United Kingdom alone.

International investment raises particular challenges in terms of corporate disclosure, regulatory structures, environmental standards and differing national and cultural priorities. For example, foreign companies, particularly those based in developing countries, may not have the same social and environmental standards as companies in developed countries. Nevertheless, there is growing pressure for financial institutions in both developing and advanced countries to consider the social and environmental implications of their investment decisions.

Defining social responsibility

As more insurers, pension funds and banks seek to build reputations for socially responsible investing (SRI), there is a growing demand for fund managers to consider the social and environmental impact of the companies in which they are investing. Socially responsible fund managers generally only invest in companies that can pass ethical screens that award high marks for good labour relations, charitable contributions, and a pro-active environmental policy, while filtering firms that are involved in tobacco, alcohol, animal testing, or nuclear power.

However, defining what constitutes a socially responsible investment is based often on subjective values and political trends that may at times give rise to contradictions between societal goals. For example, investments in defence/weapons companies may be considered socially irresponsible, yet consumers benefit from the peace provided by a strong and deterrent defence force. Investments by pharmaceutical companies are also in an ambiguous position, as there are those that question if they should be included in a SRI fund because they help to save lives, or whether they should be excluded because they experiment on animals.

Societies and people within them have different social values, and thus reaching a consensus about what constitutes 'social responsibility' is not an easy task. Ethics are subjective, so while a conservative from the US Mid-West probably does not share the same values as a liberal activist from San Francisco, there is also the issue of industrial sectors being systematically classified as 'bad'. In Canada resource-based companies (timber, mining and oil production) account up over 40 per cent of the Toronto Stock Exchange; US screening standards, however, typically viewed these companies in these sectors negatively. Thus in order to comply with US standards of corporate social responsibility and to attract investments, many of these companies were forced to become leaders in revamping their environmental programmes, while offering well-paid jobs.

Gathering information on investments to foster corporate social responsibility

Gathering information about the activities of a firm's commitment to societal and environmental goals and actions is the first step in determining to what extent investment could be used to reward or sanction firms. In many cases, however, such information is scarce or is not always reliable. Part of this is because Social Research firms tend to be understaffed and possess limited resources. They often rely on data banks to scan for environmental or other irregularities, but for the most part they rely on company reports, which increases the risk that a company's social performance is not accurately assessed. In addition, most investment firms use what is called 'first level screens', meaning that they may say that they will not invest in nuclear power or defence companies, but they may not be screening banks that hold huge investments in the same industries. Banks are a popular investment of social funds, but banks are often not researched, mostly due to the complication and multiple variables involved.

Interest in socially responsible reporting was emphasised in the UK in July 2000 when an amendment to the Pensions & Investments Act came into effect. The amendment requires occupational pension plan trustees to disclose how social, environmental and ethical issues are accounted for in the investing strategies of their pension plans, including shareholder activism. A survey undertaken by Environmental Resources Management (ERM), an internal environmental consulting firm, reports that 21 of the UK's 25 largest pension funds intend to implement socially responsible investment principles. About 70% of the funds plan on implementing active engagement of companies rather than simply boycotting specific industries (tobacco or alcohol). Following a survey by the Social Investment Forum, local authority pension fund managers emerged as more socially responsible in their investment practices than their occupational equivalents.

In Germany an umbrella organisation for ethical and ecological investment was created this year for investment in German speaking countries. Founded at the 'Green Money' Fair in Berlin, it is the first central forum on this issue in Germany. The aim of the forum is to promote and disseminate green investment, with focus on social and ecological disclosure regulation provided by a new German law on pension funds that states that providers must give written information explaining how the ethical, social and legal matters were considered when using fees. Well known investment firms, rating agencies, and several innovative companies that are concerned about using 'green capital' are among the 28 founding members of the forum.

The EC sees this as a distinct challenge. Despite the fact that there are already operations in place Member states and there are already a number of rating agencies with well developed methodologies determined to meet the local demand, there is not a common European approach or a clear mechanism for identifying socially responsible companies. No measures are in place or indicators agreed upon or operational and although there is no intention to replace all existing methodologies in place, they are seeking an agreed methodology that can be used for a European investment market.

Although there is still much to overcome, progress is being made. CSR Europe's Programme on Communication and Reporting was created in 1998 in order to respond to the growing need for know-how on reporting in the business sector. The CSR matrix was developed as a tool to encourage companies to share best practice, benchmark and evaluate their performance. The possibility of working together in a common methodology was demonstrated in November 2000 in Brussels, where European rating agencies joined together in order to provide analysis of 45 companies. The EC hope to facilitate the collaboration between experts in this field and effectively establish a single methodology for European-wide investments. The ultimate goal of the EC is to move towards the direction of having a European social index.

Prior to this, socially responsible investing was primarily motivated by the social, environmental and ethical concerns of individual and private investors. The EC tends to believe that it is premature to consider establishing legislation in this area on a European scale, as the Commission fears that legislation will reinforce standard practice, not the much sought after best practice. As an alternative to legislation, the commission is seeking to raise awareness and identify best practice, while encouraging the development of a framework for social reporting. With this new amendment in the UK however, for the first time financial institutions are being used as a key policy instrument to bring about sustainable development. Internationally, if fund managers can agree upon standards, then they could become an important benchmark for the industry, giving companies a more precise idea of what is expected and pressuring on them to improve their performance.

Social indices

Social indices are rigorously constructed measurements to benchmark the social and environmental performance of companies. In order for an index to work as an investment benchmark, it must provide an unbiased model of the market segment that it is intended to represent and should be as representative as possible of the underlying market, both in terms of market capitalisation and industry coverage. The following section reviews several indices in use in OECD countries.

The Domini 400 Social Index

The Domini 400 Social Index (DSI) was devised and launched in 1990 to measure performance of socially screened stocks. It is the oldest socially and environmentally screened index in the US. Domini Social Investments is one of the fastest growing mutual fund companies in the US with assets at $1.5 billion in 2000, up from about $200 million three years prior. The DSI monitors the performance of 400 US corporations that pass multiple, broad-based social screens[**] and the social research firm of Kinder, Lydenberg, Domini & Co., Inc (KLD) determines the composition of the index.

The DSI was created in order to fill four needs:

- to answer the question of whether social screening carries an inherent financial cost;
- to provide a socially screened equity benchmark;
- to communicate the standards of mainstream social investors to corporations and the general public;
- to provide a basis for a screened, indexed investment tool for investors.

Through a combination of exclusionary and qualitative screens, KLD began screening the companies listed in Standard & Poors 500 Index, eliminating companies that failed to qualify under their screens. About 250 companies were eliminated in the process, and then KLD began researching outside of the S&P companies. KLD aims to keep the turnover rate of the DSI to a minimum. The most obvious reason for removing a company is when it ceases to trade as a public company, but companies are also removed for social reasons. Although infrequent, this occurs if a company enters into a business excluded by the DSI screens such as gambling. If though, a company encounters some controversy in areas of the qualitative screens, such as environment, KLD will evaluate the situation and base its decision on removal

** 'Social screening' is the application of social criteria, or screens, to investment decisions on conventional investments, such as stocks, bonds and mutual funds.

or not based on the proportion of the controversy. A company that has been removed form the DSI for social reasons may not be added for at least two years.

The qualitative screening criterion contains attributes that are listed as strengths that KLD seeks in a company to be added to the Index.

Community strengths:

- The company has given over 1.5% of trailing net earnings before taxes to charity or has been very generous its giving on a consistent basis;

- The company has a notably innovative giving programme that supports non-profit organisations such as those promoting self-sufficiency among economically disadvantaged.

- The company is a participant in public/private partnerships that support housing initiatives for the disadvantaged populations.

Inversely, concerns in the same area could be that the company is a financial institution whose local investment practices have led to controversies. Another concern could be that company has engaged in actions that produced major controversies concerning its economic impact on the community (environmental contamination, plant closings or anything else that would affect the quality of life in the community).

Diversity strengths:

- The company's chief executive officer is a woman of from a minority group;

- The company hires woman and minorities and promotes them to responsible positions in the firm, with woman or minorities amongst the high line officers or are responsible for overseeing operations that account for 20 per cent of the company's revenues;

- Woman, minorities, and /or the disabled hold seats of the board of directors;

- The company has outstanding employee benefits;

- The company does at least 5 per cent of its subcontracting with woman or minority-owned businesses.

- The company has implemented innovative hiring programmes or human resource programmes for the disabled, or has a good reputation for employing the disabled.

- The company has implemented policies regarding gay and lesbian employees (such as benefits for same-sex domestic partners.

Concerns in this area would be that a company has recently been involved with affirmative action controversies or that a company has no woman on its board of directors or amongst its senior line managers.

The FTSE Index

The FTSE, a UK-based stock market index firm, introduced new indices, FTSE4Good, to help establish a global standard for socially responsible investing. These indices were developed in association with the Ethical Investment Research Service[3] (EIRIS), and will be weighted by market capitalisation and will consist of a tradable and a benchmark index for four areas: the UK, Europe, the US, and the rest of the world. The indices can serve as the basis for mutual or institutional funds, or for choosing stocks. The FTSE4Good is based on principles already existent in business code of conduct, such as the UN Global Compact and the OECD Guidelines for MNEs. The FTSE evaluates a company's commitment to social responsibility by examining three areas: the environment, human rights and stakeholder relationships. The indices will only include companies that are progressing toward a best practice model for each area. Firms engaged in controversial activities will be excluded from FTSE4Good. Over 50 per cent of eligible companies may fail to be included in FTSE4GOOD due to lack of data. The FTSE and EIRIS are working with companies to gather this information in order to overcome the problem.

Social accounting

The social accounting movement has European roots and rests on the premise that companies should account for social activities in the same way as for financial activities. It is a voluntary, systematic, auditing process for companies and organisations to measure their social achievements and ethical values. It entails costs, both monetary and time, but it is an important exercise that should be encouraged. It enables a company to re-evaluate its objectives, clarify its values and the way in which they are communicated to stakeholders, and develop time-plans, budgets and task allocations in order to find solutions to increase profits while improving environmental protection and fulfilling social goals.

The basis of this method entails:

- setting the precise social objectives of the company;
- formulating indicators to benchmark the stated objective;
- identifying all stakeholders;
- filling in questionnaires;
- drawing a sample of interviews;
- collecting and analysing data;
- writing a final report.

By confronting aspects of accountability in a positive manner, a company enhances its reputation for living its values, while at the same time improving the quality of life for both internal and external stakeholders. Report findings and recommendations could be very useful to the community at large and local authorities. Currently, social accounting is only regulated in France where companies with over 300 employees are expected to produce a *Bilan Social.* The use of the method is progressing however, as companies realise that measuring social impact is a necessary component in being a good corporate citizen.

Shareholder activism

A development in the 1990s in the market for corporate control has been an approach called shareholder activism, in which socially responsible investors engage in direct dialogue with company management. Socially responsible investors can protect the integrity of their investment by becoming active shareholders within the company. These institutions have pressured board members and managers of many leading corporations to improve performance and to remove anti-takeover obstacles. Since corporations operate on a one-share-one-vote principle, this permits every shareholder of the company to bring up questions about social issues and file shareholder resolutions. If a shareholder's resolution gains enough support, it can be brought to a proxy vote; if it wins, the company can be forced to reverse its objectionable policy, but in most cases, filers of social issue resolutions do not expect things to go that far. In reality, the filers use this as a tool to get management's attention and to raise the issue. It is a sort of financial lobbying.

Although share boycotting (the boycotting of stock in companies in order to reduce the price of its shares so as to force change) may appear useful, the most successful way to advance is through active engagement. While publicly institutional investors have frequently joined dissident shareholders in voting against management on proxy proposals, privately, they have engaged management in discussions about ways of improving performance. They may also have an effect by sponsoring or participating in shareholder actions, so that ethical investors take more direct roles in changing corporate behaviour. Institutional investors have been successful in forcing divestitures, CEO turnover and change in governance structure in a number of prominent corporations (examples have been with General Motors and IBM). The Coalition for Environmentally Responsible Economies (CERES) in the US, for example, has considerably advanced the environmental agenda by persuading companies to sign a set of principles and bringing corporations together to discuss accountability. This type of advocacy has grown popular in recent years as shareholder resolutions more than doubled in two years.

However, some business leaders and politicians have argued that large pension funds lack the expertise and ability to serve as effective monitors in the market for corporate control.

Social and environmental ratings

Social and environmental rating promotes and provides social investment research and investment products. Social rating agencies follow financial markets and prepare profiles of publicly traded companies, promoting and developing socially screened national and trans-national financial indices. In Europe, a growing number of individual and institutional investors seek to evaluate the social performance of companies that they have stock in. For example in France, the rating agency Arèse uses investment criteria covering human resources, environment, suppliers/customers, shareholders, and the community. The community criterion entails a survey of the partnerships set-up by the company with stakeholder in the country or locality it is operating in and focuses specifically on: humanitarian sponsorship, social sponsorship, environmental sponsorship, local development and art and sport sponsorship. In addition to information gathering in companies, Arèse also attempts to raise awareness on social responsibility to the companies in question, and encourages companies to engage in partnerships wherever they have a local presence, promoting sustainable development.

Arèse, KLD, and eight other firms in Europe and Canada are members of the SIRI Group. SIRI stands for Sustainable Investment Research International Group and the members of the SIRI Group agree upon producing company profiles of the leading European and North American companies by market capitalisation (indexes, FTSE for example). Each partner is responsible for drafting company profiles based on the most accurate social and environmental data they can find. All members use the same methods and have access to information on each screened company, allowing for an accurate sector-based approach of the rating system, with a complete overview of international competition. The aim of the SIRI Group is to find a local partner for every screened country, and to raise awareness and promote responsible investing on all continents. The group will expand into Asia and South Africa by the end of 2001.

Ultimately, these evaluation processes, as well as being useful for investors and the companies, should be used as a vehicle to advancing public policy on the issue of CSR.

Box 11. Council on Economic Priorities: Shopping for a better world

The Council on Economic priorities (CEP) is a public research organisation for impartial analysis of social and environmental records of corporations. CEP is committed to making information on corporate social responsibility available to millions of consumers, investors, policy makers and business.

Created in 1969, CEP grades overall company performance, not the performance of specific products or specific subsidiaries. Information comes from company surveys and independent sources and covers human rights, equal employment opportunity, concern for the environment and community involvement, but also animal welfare, gay and lesbian issues, and military involvement. Companies are graded in comparison to other in the CEP database of Fortune 500 companies, therefore an ‘A’ grade does not automatically mean that the company is responsible in all areas, but that it is superior to the other companies being tracked. CEP’s analysis shows that companies with a good record of ethical decision-making will do better in the marketplace by demonstrating good corporate citizenship.

Box 11 (*cont.*)

CEP mobilises and informs consumers to make more informed choices, empowering them to select the companies whose policies and practices they support. Since 1988, CEP has been publishing SHOPPING FOR A BETTER WORLD, a guide that rates over 200 companies with over 2 100 brand names in 23 product categories. Over a million copies have been sold, assisting the concerned consumer to purchase products that will protect the environment, fight child, support equal rights for minorities and women.

Social labelling

Social labelling is often considered when discussing financial concerns and CSR because of the economic component involved. Social labels are intended to inform consumers about the social conditions of production, in order to assure them that the item they are purchasing was produced under fair and equitable working conditions. The proponents of many social labelling initiatives are trying to initiate change by starting from the consumer and moving back through the marketing chain to affect modes of production. In the example of child labour, these labelling initiatives usually have the aim of also directly contributing to the improvements in the situation of child labourers and their families and the communities by setting up local projects financed through the labelling initiative itself.

Social labelling is often referred to as voluntary because the label is put in place by a producer or whole-saler by choice, rather than in response to government legislation or import requirements. Social labelling has been advocated and advanced mainly by groups and organisations which are concerned with poor working and living conditions, mostly in developing countries where many of the products are produced and then exported to industrialised countries. An example of voluntary social labels in an industrialised country is the 'union label' that still exists in a modified form, but was in widespread use in the US before clothing began to be manufactured in volume overseas. The label was sewn in every garment manufactured by members of a large American trade union, The International Ladies' Garment Workers' Union.

All social labelling initiatives share some common features:

- The physical labelling of certain products by either the use of a descriptive label or a logo that has a specific social meaning for its sponsors. The label implies that certain standards have been met.

- The labelling initiatives necessitate outreach towards consumers, communicating the social implications of purchasing labelled products.

- The labelling initiative collects funds from the retailers or importers of the products in order to improve specific conditions in the region of production. This usually represents a very small percentage of the sales volume or import volume of the product, and may increase the actual unit price of the product to consumers by up to 2 per cent.

In both Europe and the US, labelling initiatives have arisen in food importing in recent years. This involves directly purchasing from small farmers at generous prices and then repackaging the products in various countries under specific trademarks or labels. These 'fair trade' products, as they are collectively called, have made notable progress in some European countries, achieving up to 4 per cent of the total national market for certain commodities (so some money is re-channelled back into local regions). Consumer choice can act as a critical lever in improving conditions for disadvantaged populations. Labelled products are those that have been produced under better conditions.

A social labelling initiative can have a substantial effect on production practices in an entire export industry in a large country. The label that consumers are encouraged to purchase carries economic and social consequences. The success of social labelling rest on the consumers' willingness to prefer labelled over unlabelled products. The public perceives the label as a guarantee of 'politically correct' economic and social behaviour and informal surveys in the US and Europe indicate consumer willingness to bear the slightly higher costs of socially labelled products.

Community investing

Community investing is the sector of SRI that has the most direct impact on communities. Community investment capital flows into non-profit loan funds and community development banks, credit unions, corporations and programmes both domestically and internationally. Investors are also enabling local non-profits and small businesses to maintain facilities. Investment opportunities vary widely in terms, rates, and risk, but effect of community investing is direct and measurable. The four primary sectors of lending that community investing supports include affordable housing, micro-enterprise, small business and community development.

Financial services are critical for healthy local economies and without them, individuals become financially excluded and businesses struggle to survive meaning fewer jobs and local goods and services for the local community. The community finance sector aims to increase the accessibility of appropriate finance for individuals, businesses and social enterprises and thus strengthen and revitalise local communities. The sector is made up of a range of Community Finance Initiatives (CFIs), including community loan funds, micro-credit funds, and community area regeneration trusts. They are politically independent and are often combined with forms of community ownership and/or engagement.

Traditionally, British banks have resisted the US model for social investment in distressed communities, but this is changing. In 1999, the UK government put pressure on banks to disclose how much business they do in distressed communities, calling for greater transparency, in order to stimulate private sector engagement in these areas. This year, a new national index was launched that tracks the success of micro and small businesses in UK inner cities. The index, Inner City 100, was devised by the New Economy Foundation (NEF), and is backed by the Royal Bank of Scotland and NatWest. The New Economics Foundation has been engaged in developing national policy for community finance, and has pioneered practical community finance initiatives like the London Rebuilding Society. It also brings extensive experience of micro-finance in developing countries.

November 2000 in the UK the Social Investment Task Force made some recommendations in a bid to find new ways of increasing the flow of investment into poorer areas. They investigated a range of new initiatives, and came up with five proposals:

- A community investment tax credit to encourage people and companies to invest in community development. The programme would invest £1 billion in profit-seeking and not-for-profit enterprises in deprived communities.
- Community development venture funds: they suggest a matched funding partnership between the government on the one hand and the venture capital industry, entrepreneurs, institutional investors and banks on the other. They suggest that £100 million should be

made available from the government in matched funding during the duration of the programme.

- Disclosure of where individual banks are lending their money in under-invested communities.
- Greater latitude and encouragement for charitable trust and foundations to invest in community development activities, even where these include a significant for-profit element.
- Support for community development financial institutions, including community banks, community loan funds, micro-loan funds and community development venture funds.

This requires action by the government and agencies like the Small Business Service, the private sector and the voluntary sector. The NEF calculations indicate that more than 100 000 jobs could be created within the next five years if the proposed Community Investment Tax Credit is implemented and would serve as a first step for using the tax code for socially responsible market activity.

Box 12. London's new mutual finance institution

The London Rebuilding Society (LRS) is London's new mutual finance institution. It was created to provide support to social enterprises in London and to foster social inclusion and regeneration.

LRS will lend to viable non-bankable social enterprises putting something back into London's poorer communities. LRS will lend to enterprises with social aims, using their surpluses for the benefit of employees, consumers, the local community, engage in community reinvestment. LRS will provide:

- loans for social enterprises through the Social Enterprise Fund;
- small low-interest loans for charities and voluntary organisations;
- and loans for energy saving activities.

People living and working in London and organisations working for London, as well as borrowers, will be LRS members and owners.

LRS funds will come from the public and private sectors and from a share issue. Various trusts and foundations have supported early development and funds have been provided from Industrial Common Ownership Finance and NatWest. As a mutual institution, LRS will have a share issue to raise equity in 2001.

The Community Development Financial Institute (CDFI) in the US is a private sector financial intermediary that has community development as its primary mission and develops a range of programmes and methods to meet the needs of low-income neighbourhoods. Started in 1999, they are market-driven and locally controlled and he CDFIs use credit rather than charity as an effective tool to build wealth in distressed areas. Funding comes from private and public sources, with private sector funds coming from corporations, individuals, and private foundations. CDFIs work in partnership with traditional financial institutions to channel private investment into underdeveloped communities, either through direct investment in the CDFI or through co-ordination of lending, investment and other services. Start-up financing is provided to entrepreneurs for risky investments in distressed areas, ranging from day-care centres to beauty salons.

CDFIs range from small non-profit micro-enterprise lenders, to larger banking institutions (Self-Help Credit union example) with thousands of borrowers and loans; size being irrelevant, all CDFIs are about putting community investment capital to work. CDFIs fall into several categories and offer varying investment opportunities:

1. Community Development Banks (CDBs) are for-profit entities that target disadvantaged communities to provide banking service, loans and revitalisation programmes. In the US, there are only a few.

2. Community Development Credit Unions (CDCUs) are non-profit, regulated and insured, serving their members in low-income communities (e.g., Self-Help, see Box 13). There are over 200 in the US.

3. Community Development Loan Funds (CDLFs) are non-profit, unregulated and uninsured, administering loan funds for community development and various lending activities, including the environment, housing, small business, funding facilities for non-profits. CDLFs are able to make loans that banks and credit unions would probably avoid, and often include technical assistance with capital. Many CDLFs accept private investment. Offerings tied to be below the market rate, between 0-5 per cent for 1-5 years;

Box 13. Self-Help Credit Union: creating ownership opportunities

Self-Help (a CDFI) was created in 1980 as a community development lender serving home buyers, small business and non-profits across North Carolina. Self-Help has provided over $1 billion in financing to over 16 000 families, businesses, and non-profit organisations, helping those who are under-served by traditional lenders through the support of socially responsible citizens and institutions across the US.

Self-Help's work is made possible by partnerships with many groups in government, business and the non-profit sector, as well as the depositors and investors who provide critical support. Today, Self-Help reaches beyond the North Carolina, assisting low-income families in 42 states.

Self-Help lending is targeted to minorities, woman, rural residents and low-income families, and provides loans to first-time homeowners, entrepreneurs and non-profits. In the community service realm, Self-Help estimates that it has helped to create 13 600 jobs, 14 000 childcare spaces, 3 710 educational spaces, and 452 supportive housing spaces. Self-Help is one of the nation's largest micro-lenders, with over 50 per cent of its commercial loans made for under $25 000. Self-Help's Sustainable Development Initiative lends to environmentally focused businesses and firms in inner cities and rural town centres.

The United Nations, Presidents Ronald Reagan and Bill Clinton, as well as the Federal Reserve Banks of Atlanta and Richmond have all pointed to Self-Help as a national model for community development.

4. Community Development Corporations (CDCs) are non-profit, unregulated and uninsured, primarily involved in housing, neighbourhood revitalisation and community development. They may also have loan funds within their programmes. CDCs often develop their own umbrella of projects, funding and building a portfolio of deals.

   LISC (Local Initiatives Support Corporation) was established in 1979 by the Ford Foundation and six corporations. LISC is the United States' largest non-profit community development support organisation, with 41 local programmes working in over 100 cities and urban counties across the country, also working in neglected rural communities in 39 states and Puerto Rico. LISC mobilises partnerships to help local people rebuild deteriorated neighbourhoods and rural areas across America. It provides funding and technical know-how to CDCs and helps the CDCs to work with banks and local governments to build decent, affordable housing, improve commercial and retail services, and generate jobs and income for local residents. LISC serves as a vehicle through which the private sector gets involved in community revitalisation and through strong relationships with over 1 600 corporations, foundations and public agencies, and increasing numbers of individual donors, LISC has raised nearly $3 billion to support grassroots community revitalisation, 97 per cent of it from private sources.

5. Micro Finance Institutions (MFIs) are non-profit micro-loan institutions that are unregulated and uninsured. Grameen Bank is one of the oldest and largest examples of an MFI. Micro lending is less popular in the United States than elsewhere, but it is growing in the United States as well. MFIs often target the very poorest, offering technical assistance and using the peer-lending model.

The Grameen Bank was started in Bangladesh in 1976 as an experiment of how a small amount of credit could affect the lives of the rural poor. It has since loaned more than $2 billion to millions of people has reversed conventional banking practice by removing the need for collateral and created a banking system based on mutual trust, accountability, participation and creativity. GB sees credit as a cost-effective weapon against poverty and it serves as a catalyst in the overall development of socio-economic conditions of the poor. GB's positive impact on its poor and formerly poor borrowers has been documented in many independent studies carried out by external agencies including the World Bank, the International Food Research Policy Institute (IFPRI) and the Bangladesh Institute of Development Studies.

More than 4 000 people from 100 countries have gone through Grameen's training/exposure programmes over the last 10 years. Some have returned to their countries and replicated the GB financial system to help the poor people in their country to overcome poverty. Over 80 institutions worldwide operate micro-credit programmes based on the Grameen methodology, providing credit to several hundred thousand poor borrowers worldwide. Of these institutions, 80 are receiving funding from Grameen Trust.

For all CDFIs, there is a set term of investment, but early withdrawal may be possible with some penalties against interest of principle.

There are three options available on how to actually make the investment:

1. Direct investment: Community Development Banks and Credit Unions offer insured accounts, while only some Loan Funds, CDCs and MFIs offer uninsured investment notes. Rates range from 0-5 per cent with terms of 1-5 years.

2. Community Investment Portfolios: these are intermediary facilities allowing for the purchase of a note that is a piece of a larger pool of CDFI investments. Terms are similar to those of the CDLFs, CDCs and MFIs they invest in.

3. Mutual Funds: several mutual funds have a community investment component built right in. Mutual funds can be held in brokerage accounts, but the commitment to community investment may be very small, so not the most recommended choice for community investment.

Today, there are more than 40 mutual funds in the US and 12 in Canada that use some form of positive or negative screens. They hold upward of $13 billion, with another $3 billion invested in targeted social investments such as community development banks. In community investment, the slightly lower rate of financial return is the trade off for a higher social return.

Individual Learning Accounts and Individual Development Accounts

The Individual Learning Account (ILA) is a way of helping employees to pay for learning and their personal development. In these programmes, both the employee and the employer, and sometimes the Government, contribute money to a bank or company account in the employee's name that the employee may use for education and training. Before dispersing funds from an account, a bank or a company official makes sure that the money will be used for its intended purpose. It is mostly used in Europe and the UK, although in the US this approach may also be used to meet employee-training needs and to support lifelong learning.

Individual Development Accounts (IDAs) are a policy tool to encourage and enable low-income families to build assets for economic well-being. IDAs are matched saving accounts, where contributions for lower income participants are matched using both private and public sources. IDA programmes currently operate in about 250 communities in the US, all with different programme requirements, some characteristics remain fairly constant from one programme to the next. Individuals who participate in the programme are at or below the poverty line and must attend courses on money management and economic literacy training in order to help them in establishing budgets and cleaning up their credit. The accounts are managed by community organisations and a non-profit organisation generally recruits participants. The accounts are held in local financial institutions. The use of the IDA savings is restricted to post secondary education and training, business capitalisation, and home ownership.

Box 14. ShoreBank

The ShoreBank is the oldest and largest community development bank in the US. Founded in 1973, their mission has been to provide innovative loan, deposit and investment products while maintaining strong financial performance.

Investors from all over the US have joined ShoreBank as Development Depositors, meaning that these deposits are directed uniquely towards urban development. ShoreBank strives to connect lower income families to the mainstream economy by providing employment services, creating jobs through business lending, and providing the knowledge and financial tools necessary to purchase homes or start a business.

Over 3 000 individuals, corporations, foundations and non-profits have opened accounts at ShoreBank because of its desire to serve the local community. The Domini Money Market Account (for socially responsible investments) places investors' funds with the ShoreBank, as the social benefits of depositing directly into this bank account away those that could be offered through conventional money market products.

ShoreBank has been profitable every year since 1975, receiving national and international recognition for its efforts and has expanded activities to other states as well as developing nations, such as Pakistan, Kenya and Bangladesh.

Savings banks

Since the first savings bank was founded bank in Scotland in 1810, they have a long tradition of contributing to the local community. Traditionally, savings banks have no stockholders and the bank's assets are administered solely for the benefit of its current and future depositors. Historically, social commitment, links to regional and local authorities, and close business relations were the common elements to savings bank development in all countries.

In modern times, savings banks ensure socially responsible business dealings in the local market, primarily serving the banking needs of households and SMEs. Across Europe savings banks have created venture capital companies to help finance small firms. In Spain, France, and Germany, savings banks have created bank branches to provide tailored service to SME needs. The German savings banks association launched a programme in partnership with other business organisations to assist small firms, and in co-operation with the journal '*Stern*' and the management consulting firm McKinsey, it has launched 'Start Up', a competition for the founding companies, with prizes such as money and free consulting. In Italy, where saving banks have a long tradition of supporting SMEs, they have strengthened their role by providing high quality services with excellent advantages, such as low-interest loans for start-ups and youth entrepreneurship.

The networks maintained allow for strong bonds with the local community, and a substantial part of the savings is frequently re-routed into regional investments. Representatives and regional authorities often sit on the board of saving banks and ensure that business decisions fit with local and regional interests. The savings banks foster social cohesion through the provision of education and information, ethical investment funds, housing schemes for low-income families, involvement in environmental projects, donations to community cultural and sporting activities, and providing access to their services to everyone in the community. Spanish savings banks promote inclusion by ensuring that a third of their branches be located in towns with very low populations (less than 10 000 inhabitants). French savings banks financially contribute through projects concerning illiteracy, old age, and exclusion due to the loss of work through 'Ensemble prévenir l'exclusion', an intermediary of the Savings Banks Foundation.

During the 1980s, savings banks began providing services similar to commercial banks (checking account, credit card services, and loans) which made its role in the community's financial structure even more important. Moreover, because of the regulatory structure that the banks adhere to, they are very concerned about corporate image at the local level and are sensitive to issues of compliance and suitability. North American banks have a long tradition of community participation, and in Canada, banks and their employees are among the top corporate donors to charities and non-profit organisations. One interesting initiative that they carry out involves the use of an 'affinity card'. With credit produced in affiliation with charities and non-profit groups, affinity cards channel funds to good causes. Each time the card is used, money is directed to the designated organisation.

The European Savings Banks Group (ESBG) in Brussels has been representing European savings banks, with membership in Europe including 24 countries since 1963. All of the ESBG member banks are also members of the World Savings Bank Institution (WSBI), which has 107 members from 85 countries, co-operating internationally. The ESBG published the brochure, *Building a Europe of the Future - European Savings Banks: At the Crossroads between the Local and Global Economy*, following the Lisbon Summit of March 2000 in order to mark the turning point for the European social agenda in the banking sector and to demonstrate that the European savings banks are in solidarity with the local and regional communities in which they operate. Their role as a socially responsible credit institution with transferable activities will greatly assist the European Union in meeting its challenges. Savings banks have the ability to regulate themselves and adopted a code of conduct in 1996 establishing commitments to fair, transparent and open relationships with clients, setting the tone for simplification and clarity of financial services in the European market.

Conclusions

Finance plays a strategic role in promoting economic development and social cohesion. Financial initiatives can encourage companies and banks to support sustainable development, advance global equity and foster partnerships amongst different sectors. Increasingly investment carries the voice and values of companies, shareholders, and consumers and the impact of financial decisions on the community is tremendous. Savings banks and community development institutions also contribute to elevating the quality of life for disadvantaged communities and individuals. These institutions can fulfil their role of being socially responsible on the local level due to their close relationship with local business and local authorities for the betterment of the community.

The 2000 National Business Ethics Survey in the US confirmed earlier studies that externally imposed regulation on business can be invasive and inefficient and evidence is accumulating that ethics programmes are more successful when stakeholders see them as focusing on values and not about compliance. Companies reason that if they can substitute moral persuasion for inefficient regulation, then they will benefit. Following an ethical programme is good for business, but choosing the right programme leads to further questions. And the very definition of 'ethical', by nature subjective, adds to sensitivities on the subject. Social indices, both those in existence and those recently put into place, are advancing the debate, clarifying the rules for companies and indirectly pressuring them to adhere to standards. Social accounting systems can assist companies find the best path to adhering to high social standards.

The SRI movement is gaining momentum, and it appears to be clear that this sort of investment will become mainstream in the future so long as reporting systems evolve. If 'good business practices make good companies', then maybe examining employee relations policies should be done prior to any investing, following the rational that companies that treat their employees well will find that their employees will treat their customers well, and will ultimately treat their investors well. So, perhaps in the long-term, when using the term 'ethical', what really matters is whether a company relates to its employees, its customers and other stakeholders groups in a way that meets their expectations, both ethical and financial. Fund managers should place more emphasis on how companies manage these relations.

Developing a global framework for ethical investing in order to exchange best practice in the financial sector is not an easy task. Through the exchange of views and the identification of common guidelines, the OECD can help provide norms for social investing. Critics argue that improvement is necessary if social screens are to have a large impact on corporate behaviour. Others argue that SRI is politics by other means. It is aimed at achieving results and is a tool used to effect change in publicly traded corporations. But significant reforms can be achieved when all factors that can affect a company or industry's image are combined. This includes corporate governance, environmental reporting standards, changing consumer buying habits, and opening companies to more critical scrutiny of their social practices. By using ethical guidelines to choose investments and by raising issues of social concern with the companies they work with, social investors are redefining the corporate bottom line.

NOTES

3. EIRIS is an independent provider of research on corporate social, environmental and ethical performance.

PRESENTATIONS BY SPEAKERS

OF THE THIRD PART OF THE ROUNDTABLE DISCUSSIONS

LINKING ETHICS AND FINANCE

TO FOSTER SOCIAL RESPONSIBILITY

Saving Banks Serving the Community

Adriana Alvarez, Member of the Management Committee, European Savings Banks Group

The European Saving Banks Group

I represent the European Savings Banks Group in Brussels as well as the World Savings Banks Institute. We have a European group representing 24 countries in Europe and a worldwide group that represents 115 countries worldwide. There are financial institutions, savings banks, as well as a wider group of institutions that we know in Europe including Caisses d'épargnes, savings banks, German Sparkasse, Cassa d'Espagne, etc.

Worldwide we cover a group that has a number of things that bind us together very strongly. I would like to explain what these features are and how we operate. The feature that unites savings banks across the globe is the fact that they are small, decentralised, locally based, regionally focused credit institutions. They are different legal entities. They can be co-operatives, they can be mutually held in other ways, they can be publicly held, some are now owned by foundations. Others have recently privatised and are full private entities incorporated under national corporate law rules, etc., but what binds us together is that we are the smaller, decentralised institutions that are retail banks and we focus very much on the SME market.

The interest in making a presentation here today is to demonstrate to you what binds us together. We believe in co-operations across borders. Our goal is not to merge, or to take over other banks, we remain focused on our local market, but at the same can learn from other regions and countries. Working groups in Brussels and across the world interact through the various seminars held on these issues. We promote the exchange of best practise. A valuable part of global co-operation amongst these savings banks depends on the transmission of information at our international seminars, where information is exchanged on technical assistance, housing financing, SME financing, start-up capital, etc. All of these seminars reach our Latin American, African, and Asian members and we have a separate group in Europe that works with the Central European countries (CEC). There really is a need to focus on assistance to the banks in CEC areas for varying reasons ranging from rules of conduct, transfer of knowledge, or because they are experiencing difficulties and require technical assistance from the ESBG.

The role of the savings bank in the global economy

The organisations of today's conference is timely, as a brochure has just been published *Building a Europe of the Future -- European Savings Banks At Crossroads between the Local and Global Economy.* This brochure explains that we are not only banks and credit institutions in the local market, but that what do we extend past that. Our special role is ensuring that savings banks do indeed exercise a true responsibility to ensure socially responsible business dealings.

This is not a new concept, as savings banks were born in the age of enlightenment and history has created these entities as institutions that are supposed to group together the local authorities, local business. They implicitly sought not to have the classic corporate holding that is customary to most corporate entities and their shareholders. We believe in working together with our stakeholders, who are not only our clients, but also the local authorities and local business in the community. The ESBG fulfils its role of being a socially responsible credit institution in four specific areas:

- Close involvement in local and regional economy;
- Ensure the responsibility for the community;
- Lend to the local public sector;
- Financial focus on SMEs and micro-enterprise.

Although I will focus on our European activity, all is completely applicable and transferable to our members worldwide. As for the first area mentioned, our close involvement in the local and regional economy is achieved through working together with local authorities and local municipalities. There is a lot of financing through and with these local authorities. Deposits from these local authorities can range between 40-60 per cent in some countries; Germany is 60% for example. These deposits are held with us because we work with the local authorities to re-invest the deposits into local projects. We work with the local authorities on specific employment projects, tax relief programmes, and generally on the development of financing schemes for local projects.

The second area touches upon the need for strong social responsibility to the local community. Some of our members are obliged to fulfil certain responsibilities based on legislation in their region. For example, Spanish savings banks are required under law to give 25 per cent of their profits to the Obra Social (Social Works). The Obra Social can be anything from starting up local business to financing projects to refurbish schools to modernising museums, or even to work on local art or other novelty projects. French savings banks have also added local legislation that they must now act in the *intérêt général*, meaning that they allocate about 10 per cent of their profits to local projects. German savings banks have *öffentlichen Auftrag* (a kind of public mandate) and an open account for everyone, and that is their way of fulfilling their responsibility to the community. There examples demonstrate that responsibility is carried out in different ways, we do not have a single system that we think should be applied to all concerned, but these different projects work very well in their individual country, community, or locality.

Promoting SMEs

The third area, lending to the local public sector is important, but I will skip over that to go directly to the forth are of interest concerning SMEs and micro-enterprises. In Europe, most savings banks have the largest share of the market in financing SMEs. Since they are small and since they are local and decentralised, these banks have a very thorough understanding of the needs of local SMEs. Due to the conclusions of the Lisbon Summit, the brochure *Building a Europe of the Future -- European Savings Banks At Crossroads between the Local and Global Economy* was produced in order to demonstrate how we finance SMEs and how that adds to local employment. The World Savings Bank Institution actually focuses more on establishing micro-credits than in working with SMEs. Although related work, the micro-credits represent much smaller funds for much smaller companies and projects.

In Europe, we work closely with SMEs through the European Union and the SME Roundtable. We have an international correspondent network for the dissemination of information on SMEs, which allows for the exchange of information of best practise where each member of our European can easily exchange information and best practise amongst each other. Different countries have installed networks to either help SMEs with start-ups or to actually open up special branches of saving banks. In Spain they only work with the SMEs and have a full focus on those needs. We have a group based in Paris, EURO-SOFAC that is a European consultancy and social assistance providing para-banking services to SMEs and promoting international activities. To date, EURO-SOFAC has developed activities with companies from 25 countries in more than 30 economic sectors.

We try to help SMEs concretely in order to foster local employment through out network. SMEs that are having problems dealing or selling across borders may contact out international contacts in their field of business for assistance. We do not have precise statistics in this widely decentralised network, but the numbers for the 24 countries in Europe can be found at the back of the above mentioned brochure. It gives an interesting overview of the strengths of the savings banks.

Responsible Investing: Focus on Sustainable Development

Geneviève Ferone, Director General, Arèse

I am the General Manager of Arèse, a social rating firm, listed on the French stock market. Arèse was created 3 years ago in order to evaluate and rate firms on social and environmental criteria. Arèse's core activity is to provide in-depth analysis and ratings on corporate social responsibility and sustainable development issues. Such assessment is used in long term investment strategies and enables the development of socially responsible funds that take into account social and environmental criteria in addition to financial analysis.

We have two sorts of clients: institutional investors with a long term outlook wishing to obtain information on social and environmental performances about companies they invest in and money managers willing to tailor specific investment universe and fund, combining this non-financial information with other financial data.

Arèse is not a research centre on corporate social responsibility. Nor are we consultants to help improve the behaviour of an enterprise. We are not lobbyists, and we are not a forum for socially responsible investing in France. Although our function of rating firms socially and environmentally for investors may seem ambiguous, it requires a rigorous methodology and there are very few standards in this field, whereas in the financial sector, the standards are well known and clearly defined.

Investing responsibly

This is a young debate and I think that the financial market is becoming more and more aware of the issues we deal with. When choosing an investment fund or strategies, it is evident that the historical tendency of the social and environmental behaviour of an enterprise emerges, and this information will be integrated to the model for investments. In France, we have contributed to the launching of more than 20 investment funds. Our clients include the biggest French banks, Société Générale, the Banque Nationale de

France, as well as autonomous and independent money management firms. We contributed to the launching of funds for traditional institutions like the Caisses de retraites, as well as private ethical funds and there is no doubt that the financial community is showing interest in these new criteria for social and environmental issues.

Researching companies: a systematic approach

When researching a company in order to obtain information to form an evaluation, we try to establish a dialogue with them in order to promote social responsibility. We need to know what the notion of social responsibility means in their country, whether the locality they are in is their home base or whether it is a subsidiary or implantation, we need information on labour laws, the environment, the production chain, and the supply chain.

Geographically, there are certain issues more prevalent in some regions than others. If I say Bangladesh, you will certainly think of child labour. If I say Mali, you will most likely think of forced labour and human rights problems.

There is a triple orientation of our research:

1. Sectoral, where the social responsibly of an enterprise and the challenges faced varies according to their sector of activity. A firm working in construction will surely face different issues than CAP Gemini, for example.

2. Geographic, some countries are more sensitive, the third world for example, and we look at how the responsibility is exposed in different parts of the world, how the notion of social responsibility is impregnated in the management of the enterprise. Throughout our observations, we note practices extremely different from one enterprise to another. American companies and companies in the United Kingdom have different methods than elsewhere concerning the subject of CSR.

3. Thematic, our criterion covers human resources, the environment, and relations with shareholders (corporate governance, relations with clients and suppliers, and the relation with the civil society.

Civil society, whether is be locally or internationally is extremely important. And for some companies it becomes complicated, as what Danone does in France only represents 20% of its turnover, thus judging Danone only on their activities on French soil is not efficient, and we need to know what they do internationally as well. The same example can be used for British Airways, or Aventis, and many others. Thus, this triple approach towards CSR, sectorially, geographically, thematically, is a systematic approach.

The social and environmental aspect

When we look at what a firm is doing, when they buy or enter a joint-venture on a local partnership level, we are attentive to the social aspect. We spend much of our efforts trying to determine what can be counted by the enterprise, and work is to come up with ratios, to develop information as quantitative as possible in order to be comparable. Arèse is not only a research centre, as we are also very attentive to local training as well as to exportation of expertise and strengthening the social ties. Through studies made by the World Bank, and the United Nations for example, we know that local training is an extraordinary vector of development, and we place a lot of importance on this as well as on questions concerning parity between men and woman, which remains rather ambiguous. Education of woman is also a valuable factor in development.

Thus, on the social scale, we ask for exact figures, ratios, everything related to training, salary practices, as the absence of legislation allows for dumping that could be disastrous, the freedom given to unions, and child labour. As for child labour, I should point out that we do not forbid this at Arèse, as we know that these are local realities that are very complicated, but we require the accounts of firms on this subject matter. We are very concerned over environmental awareness and integration of an environmental strategy by the company, as the consequences of ignoring these issues are considerable. When enterprises engage is behaviour that is potentially damaging to the environment in their overseas locations, we are highly sensitive to this issue and ask that firms supply us with information on this point as well.

Towards sustainable development

This is just an overview of how Arèse, as a social and environmental rating agency, contributes to the cause of corporate social responsibility. We attempt to raise awareness of large corporations, MNCs as well as SMEs that export. We advise them to establish partnerships wherever they have a local presence, partnerships with unions, associations, in order to create links that will allow for their companies to take on an orientation focusing on sustainable development.

The issues we are speaking about today were at one point extremely confidential and unknown to most of us. Today there are a multitude of actors willing to participate in this cause, but they are not necessarily capable of co-ordinating their efforts or to agree on which methods to use. I think that there is a strong consensus in determining a direction for CSR, and I think it would be useful to mobilise efforts so we could all advance in a much more efficient manner.

CONCLUSION

Corporate social responsibility: progress through partnerships

Globalisation has brought about rapid and fundamental changes to society and the role of business is evolving with this process. Business is not only an engine for economic growth, but it is a major player and partner with government in fostering social cohesion. By designing incentives and providing the infrastructures businesses need to operate, government can facilitate the role of business in addressing the societal challenges brought about by globalisation, helping firms become more socially responsible. In addition, the cultural institutions of a society, its religious and secular institutions, civic organisations, and NGOs are all the wellspring of social trust, and the third sector plays a critical role in establishing social trust and making market exchange possible.

The appeal made to business at the Lisbon Summit of March 2000 has effectively triggered dialogue that places more and more responsibility in the hands of the business community in the European Union. As OECD countries place more importance on public-private partnerships in order to tackle societal challenges such as exclusion, the role of the business sector has effectively been amplified. At the local level, businesses are inextricably linked with the communities they serve and large companies in particular can foster CSR among SMEs in their localities.

Strengthening corporate social responsibility will require the diffusion, access and use of information and communication technologies. New technologies can be used to spread awareness on CSR especially among smaller companies to exchange best practice information. Large telecommunication companies have the capacity to improve the infrastructure of distressed regions and act as an arbiter of communication in the economy. Access to telecommunications has already transformed the lives of many disadvantaged communities worldwide and voluntary initiatives and socially responsible practices in the telecommunications sector have been used to provide services in local communities. Across the OECD and beyond, telecommunication companies and governments partner to address issues such as education, health and environmental concerns.

Financial institutions drive the whole process of CSR and are the guardians of socially responsible investing. The role of capital resources in achieving social goals is undeniable and investment in ethical and socially responsible firms has rapidly grown in the last five years. Additional tools are being developed to measure the social and environmental responsibility of corporations and they are reacting to the pressure by becoming more transparent and accountable in their activities. The reporting of social and environmental activities by business is becoming more institutionalised in several European countries, whereas in the United States they have been advanced in this area. Efforts are underway at the EU to consolidate reporting amongst Member states, establishing a single methodology for the European investment market, with future hopes of building a European social index.

Regulation and legislation clearly can create an enabling framework, facilitating the change in attitudes in a community and to help spread best practice. Governments can encourage firms to become more socially responsible through fiscal policy and awards, providing incentives for firms to partner either among themselves or with government to address social issues, thus passing the message of CSR to the community as a whole. Governments should develop their role as mediator and foster relationships between different interest groups by endorsing and promoting best practice in order to develop and implement a coherent and integrated system. Partnerships with private enterprise should be encouraged, giving corporations a role in activities and ensuring the public interest. Governments should participate in making employment possibilities accessible by providing an infrastructure that corresponds to the needs of the individuals of the community, attracting inward-investment in their locality.

Community investments are being used at the local level as a device to revitalise communities through ownership and the establishment of healthy small businesses. The private sector, along with foundations and non-profit organisations, plays a large role in this field and new methods are being examined on both sides of the Atlantic to find innovative ways of increasing the flow of investment into disadvantaged areas. Companies, in partnership with financial institutions and government are taking responsibility to provide training and lifelong learning opportunities, working towards developing the skills of their employees and helping them to increase savings and build assets through Individual Learning Accounts and Individual Development Accounts.

Sharing values

Much of what has come to be called CSR has to do with public attitudes and perceptions. Companies have gained enormous influence through the branding of consumer products, which increasingly serves to convey messages and influence or reflect societal values. In this sense, selling a product becomes secondary to selling the experience. When people buy soaps at the Body Shop, they are really buying the experience of being aware of the environment and friendly and respective towards animals.

A growing number of companies are attaching their brand names, products, and services to cultural activities and events, sometimes taking over and managing it directly under their auspices. The first such event to receive widespread public attention was Hands Across America in 1986, billed as one of the largest participatory events. It was conceived by a non-profit cultural organisation to draw attention to world hunger. The sponsors planned a 4 000-mile human chain to stretch from the East to the West Coast of the United States. Coca-Cola joined the community and non-profit organisations and began to turn the event into a commercially sponsored and run cultural experience. Local subsidiaries of the company were active in increasing participation. Hands Across America was a pivotal event that turned corporations toward greater institutional involvement in social activities. It sent a clear signal that a new age of partnerships between business and consumers was underway. From that point on, businesses were saying that they did not just want the consumers' money, but they wanted to become involved in their lives and to share their values.

Consumer demands

Just as companies influence societal values, consumers themselves influence a company's policies and commercial strategies. Evidence from the US shows that one in five consumers report to either rewarding or punishing companies based on their social performance. While many large corporations can easily avoid public controversy because they do not sell directly to the public (as Cargill, the huge grain trader or Pou Chen, the world's biggest manufacturer of shoes, as well as the invisible subcontractor behind big Western brands, like Nike), public criticism often falls upon the very companies that have loudly claimed to be doing the 'right thing.' Some companies that are leaders in CSR, such as Ikea and Nike, have at times found themselves as lightening rods for criticism. The sporting-goods company Nike, for example, was accused of contracting work from a company that uses underage labour in

Cambodia. Nike terminated their relationship with the factory and pledged to ensure that all underage workers there would be removed from the work place and paid their base salary until they reached the legal work age. In this case consumers were able to influence labour standards in world trade. But there are developmental costs; Nike left the factory because it violated their code, but in doing so, they took jobs that provided income to workers in country rife with extreme poverty. The challenge for companies and governments is how to balance addressing consumers' concerns about issues such as labour standards and the environment with the costs and benefits of globalisation.

Until there are global generally accepted standards providing credible and comparative information about a company's social impact, this balance will remain difficult to achieve. Most governments have rejected suggestions for legislation to force companies to introduce social responsibility programmes, as the competitive pressures and the growing interest of investors in companies' reputations will alone be the driving force behind such programmes. The business sector uses voluntary initiatives in terms of management controls to respond to the non-financial pressures it faces and these initiatives have promoted the accumulation of management expertise necessary to translate ethical notions into the day-to-day operations of a company. But even with the best and most honourable intentions, because of the variations and differences in production locations between countries and suppliers, thorough monitoring and implementation of global codes of conduct can be difficult. In the near future, policy makers and companies will have to grapple with some unanswered questions: To what standards should companies and MNCs adhere? To the extent sanctions are effective, what penalties should be placed on those who refuse to observe them?

Corporate social responsibility in the 21st century

In conclusion, companies in the 21st century have some clear expectations to fulfil:

- Demonstrate their commitment to society's values and their contribution to social, environmental, and economic goals through actions;
- Protect society from the negative impacts of company operations and its products and services;
- Share the benefits of company activities with key stakeholders as well as with shareholders;

- Contribute to the regeneration of local communities;
- Work in partnership with government and the third sector for sustainable development;
- Demonstrate that the company can make more money by doing the right thing, and if necessary, reinventing its business strategy, thus reassuring stakeholders that the new behaviour will outlast good intentions.

CSR is an important part of the bottom line and will increasingly be at the heart of business in the 21st century. Consistently, companies that appear at the top of rankings, such as the Fortune 100, in terms of the being the best places to work are also the most admired companies by society. Amongst business, there should be more sharing of practical learning and constructive dialogue. Consensus building should be promoted amongst institutions and social partners and a level field of core standards should be developed upon which all companies can be measured. The companies most experienced with CSR find that it cannot be treated as an added-on characteristic of the company. CSR must become a core business value and strategy that is integrated into all aspects of the company from R&D, through sourcing raw materials and producing its products, to the use and the disposal of its products and services.

The promotion of a culture of integrity within companies is the most efficient way to influence corporate behaviour. The participants of the roundtable view CSR initiatives as a step towards global convergence of business practices, and not public relations ploys, as some critics may suggest. Once again, real CSR is about how a business is run -- values and beliefs become real when they are lived every day and no amount of corporate rhetoric can substitute for direct evidence of management's sincere and meaningful dedication to a consistent set of values. CSR is a global expectation and global problems respond to local initiatives, but they also demand global solutions and corporations need to respond in a comprehensive manner. The OECD could serve as a forum for exchanging experience with regard to the polices and practices for fostering corporate social responsibility as well as helping policy makers avoid potential pitfalls.

REFERENCES

DEAL, T. and KENNEDY, A. (1999),
The New Corporate Cultures - Revitalizing the Workplace after Downsizing, Mergers, and Reengineering, Perseus Publishing.

FRIEDMAN, T. (2000),
The Lexus and the Olive Tree - Understanding Globalization, Anchor Books Edition.

GIDDENS, A. (1998),
The Third Way - The Renewal of Social Democracy, Polity Press.

JOSEPH, E. (2000),
A Welcome Engagement: SMEs and Social Inclusion, Institute for Public Policy Research, May.

OECD (1999),
Business Incubation -- International Case Studies, OECD Publications, Paris.

OECD (2000*a*),
"Spotlight on the OECD Guidelines for Multinational Enterprises", OECD Policy Brief, OECD Observer Preview, Paris December.

OECD (2000*b*),
"Private Initiatives for Corporate Responsibility: An Analysis", document [DAF/IME(2000)21], OECD Directorate for Financial, Fiscal and Enterprise Affairs, Paris.

PARRISH, L. (2000),
Briefing Paper: "Corporate Social Responsibility in the United States", Corporation for Enterprise Development, Washington, DC, August.

RIFKIN, J. (2000),
The Age of Access: The new culture of hypercapitalism, where all of life is a paid-for experience, Jeremy P. Tarcher/Putnam.

ROBINSON, Mary (1998),
"The Business Case for Human Rights", *Visions of Ethical Business 1*, UN High Commissioner for Human Rights.

STECKEL, R., SIMONS, R., SIMONS, J. and TANEN, N. (1999),
Making Money While Making a Difference - how to profit with a non-profit partner, High Tide Press.

Internet Sites

ARESE S.A., www.arese-sa.com.

Corporate Social Responsibility Forum, www.csreurope.com

The Council on Economic Priorities, www.cepnyc.org.

European Roundtable of Industrialists, www.ert.be.

Global Reporting Initiative, Sustainability Reporting Guidelines,
www.globalreporting.org

Labelling Child Labour Products, www.cofc.edu

Levi-Strauss & Co., www.levistrauss.com.

OECD PUBLICATIONS, 2, rue André-Pascal, 75775 PARIS CEDEX 16
PRINTED IN FRANCE
(04 2001 13 1 P) ISBN 92-64-19512-2 – No. 52153 2001